FREE IN OBEDIENCE

By the Author

<><><>

A PRIVATE AND PUBLIC FAITH

INSTEAD OF DEATH

Free in Obedience

WILLIAM STRINGFELLOW

THE SEABURY PRESS
New York

ACKNOWLEDGMENTS

Some of the material used in this book was first introduced, in different forms, in *The Witness, Theology Today, Behold,* and *The Christian Century,* or in addresses or lectures at the Princeton Theological Seminary, the Pittsburgh Theological Seminary, the Fourth World Conference on Faith and Order, the Harvard Business School, the Diocese of Southern Ohio, the University of South Carolina Law School, and the Laymen's Academy for Oecumenical Studies.

Appreciation is also due to the Rev. Russell Claussen, Jeanne Russell, the Rev. David S. King, and Dr. Markus Barth for their helpful, practical, and critical assistance in the completion of this book.

Scriptural quotations are from the Revised Standard Version.

First Seabury Paperback *Edition Published 1967*
446-966-C-12.5-5

For Anthony Towne

PREFACE

◇◆◇◆◇◆◇◆◇◆◇◆◇◆◇

This book takes its themes from the Letter to the Hebrews and from the juxtaposition, in the present age, of the Church and the world. It is no attempt at minute exegesis or exhaustive scholarly commentary on Hebrews as such, but it does try to cast in terms of the contemporary lives of the churches and of Christians some of the issues exposed and addressed in the early churches and among the earlier Christians.

Questions attendant to the particular history and circumstances in which Hebrews was written and composed are, for the most part, put aside. It is not that these are unimportant questions, but the effort here is simply of a different sort. This effort reflects the confidence that this Letter deals with issues which not only confronted the several churches in the earlier times, but that these same issues face the several churches nowadays. Contemporary Christians can be enlightened by turning to Hebrews both about the situations of their predecessors and their own situations.

Or, to put it a bit differently, the Christians today *are* the Hebrews. The intention of this book is to affirm that the Word of God is for men, and the Bible has not merely relevance but, much more than that, a present vitality as the Word of God for men in these times.

Some other part of the New Testament might have been chosen with the same intention, but Hebrews is chosen in part because of the obscurity of its origins and authorship. It lacks the authority of positively identified writer or writers. Yet it was held in such esteem and received as having such authenticity as witness of the Word of God that it was included in the Canon of the New Testament. I trust the earlier Christians so much that this designation of Hebrews is enough for me to pay close and reverent attention to the Letter and to commend to others that they do the same.

The modern churches and the present-day Christians must, if they are to qualify to address and act in this world amid all the technologies, institutional powers, dehumanizing threats, frightful dangers of extermination, and ruthless idols which encompass men, trust the gospel. They must trust it enough to rely upon the discernment of those of the people of God who in preceding ages spoke and acted in their times and in the world as they knew it in the confidence that the Word which they heard and celebrated is the same Word present, uttered, and received in the world as it is now.

Turn, therefore, to Hebrews to find and examine some issues represented in the present existence of the Church in the world. But, in so doing, confess that the Word of God is God's own Word. It is integral, the same for every man and nation in every time and place: indeed, more glorious than that, it is eternal, the same in those places and times which yet are beyond our experience or comprehension but which nonetheless belong to the sovereignty **and** reign of the One who has disclosed himself as the Lord **of** this history which is familiar and commonplace to men.

WILLIAM STRINGFELLOW

Ascension Day, 1963
New York, New York

CONTENTS

❖❖❖❖❖

FREE IN OBEDIENCE

◇◇◇◇◇◇◇◇◇◇◇◇◇◇◇◇◇◇◇

In many and various ways God spoke of old to our fathers by the prophets; but in these last days he has spoken to us by a Son, whom he appointed the heir of all things, through whom also he created the world. He reflects the glory of God and bears the very stamp of his nature, upholding the universe by his word of power. When he had made purification for sins, he sat down at the right hand of the Majesty on high, having become as much superior to angels as the name he has obtained is more excellent than theirs.

Hebrews 1:1-4

◇◇◇◇◇◇◇◇◇◇◇◇◇◇◇◇◇◇◇

I. THE SCANDAL OF THE CHURCHES

◇◇◇◇◇◇◇◇◇◇◇◇◇◇◇◇

Therefore we must pay the closer attention to what we have heard, lest
we drift away from it. For if the
message declared by angels was valid
and every transgression or disobedience received a just retribution, how
shall we escape if we neglect such a
great salvation?

Hebrews 2:1-3a

◇◇◇◇◇◇◇◇◇◇◇◇◇◇◇◇

The crucifixion is the event which brings the meaning of
Christ's ministry into focus.

The Cross is the summation of Christ's ministry. His
birth and baptism by John, his preaching and healing, his
teaching and endurance of temptation, his affection for
sinners and acceptance of his own enemies, his power over
the demonic and his authority over the old law, his compassion for the whole world and his intimacy with all sorts
and conditions of men are gathered into his intercession for
the world on the Cross. He surrenders to death, and all
the woes which the world suffers this side of death are in
that event known and borne by him in the freedom of
God's power over death.

Christ is crucified in the freedom of the resurrection. He

15

submits to the Cross as a witness to the end of death's power over the world. He is crucified for our sake and for the sake of the whole world in order to show once and for all how men may be freed from bondage to death.

For the Christian who is assured this freedom in baptism and for the Church of Christ which is established in this freedom in Pentecost, the crucifixion is pre-eminently the event which brings all of the ordinary issues of existence in this world within the province of the gospel. There is no man, whatever his lot in life, beyond the outreach of the gospel or outside the range of the witness of the faithful. There is no nation or institution, no thing at all, whatever its characteristics or appearance, which is not a concern of the gospel and within the scope of the Church's mission. There is no issue or event anywhere or any time which is not addressed by the gospel and which is not a responsibility of the Body of Christ. The matters which occupy and preoccupy the daily attentions of secular existence are the issues which claim the attention of the Christian faith.

Concretely, that means that the people and the things with which an ordinary Christian comes into contact from day to day are the primary and most profound issues of his faith and practice. Concretely, in my own case, that means that the persons and issues which I confront every day as a lawyer, a citizen, and a person pose for me the real issues of what it is to be a Christian in this world. For me, the day-to-day issues are like these:

—a young, unmarried, pregnant girl—who says she is afraid to confide in either her parents or her minister—

comes to see me to find out how her unborn child can be adopted.

—a convict writes to ask if a job might be found for him so that he can be paroled from prison.

—a college student, unable to find summer work, borrows twenty dollars.

—a woman, who has found another man, wants a divorce from her alcoholic husband.

—a Negro is arrested because he protested discrimination in the city.

—a seminarian is discouraged and disillusioned about the churches and thinks he cannot and should not be ordained.

—an addict wants to get out of the city to try again to kick his habit.

—a family is about to be dispossessed from their tenement.

—somebody is lonely and just wants to talk.

These represent, in my life, the real issues of faith, just as the daily happenings in your life, whatever they may be, are the real issues of faith for you. The real issues of faith for the Church have to do not so much with the nature and structure of the ecclesiastical institutions as with illegitimate childbirth, or imprisonment, or with the problems of those who are unemployed, broke, estranged, persecuted, possessed, or harassed by the premonition of death. The real issues of faith have to do with the everyday needs of men in the world and with the care for and service of those needs, whatever they may be, for which the Church exists.

If modern men do not seem to listen to the Christian faith or regard seriously the churches it is because the churches have too often given men the impression that they do not care about men or the world. They have misled men into supposing that the Christian faith has nothing to do with the ordinary issues of daily life.

But the issues of the world's life remain the issues of the faith. No more persuasive and convicting, no more beautiful and innocent evidence of that has been beheld in this generation than the witness of Pope John XXIII, noticeably beloved by the world. He knew that the cares of the world are the responsibilities of the Church, the concerns of the faith, and, in fact, the joys of the faithful.

So he left his throne to visit the poor in the slums of Rome; he went to see the prisoners who could not come to see him; he welcomed the Jews as Joseph, their brother; he blessed a circus. He was a pious, human, and humble vicar of the Lord by being a servant of this world. All Christians throughout the Church are called to a similar and equally simple service.

THE CHURCHES AND THE CITY

Witness to the faith means loving and serving the world. The city is the frontier today for the Church in American society. If the mission of the Church in representing the gospel is to make an impact upon any sector of American life, it is to the city that the Church must turn and return.

The city is that frontier because the city not only increasingly dominates the whole of American society but indeed *is* American society. It is the place in which the realities present throughout the whole society have been congregated, concentrated, and brought into acute juxtaposition. Nearly half the population, for one thing, now actually live within the precincts of the modern urban complex. But those who live beyond those precincts do not escape the city's domination of commerce, culture, politics, and ideas.

If the social integration of races and nationalities is to be achieved in America the city will pioneer that achievement. If advanced technologies are to bring more freedom as well as more wealth to Americans, the city will be the first place to enjoy these benefits. If democratic government is a viable system for a mass society, the city will be the example of that. The city is the symbol of the American aspiration for freedom and society, the symbol—as the city has been for societies in the past—of salvation.

The city's destiny is also important to other nations, not just to America. Urbanization has begun to dominate Japan and South America, as well as North America and Western Europe, and it will predictably follow in other parts of the world as industrialization takes place. But this urbanization is most advanced in the United States, and what happens here is bound to affect decisively everyone everywhere.

Not long ago I was visited by a German Lutheran pastor who had been sent by his church to study American urbanization. He reported on the burgeoning urban society of Western Germany and said that he had come to New York because it was the most highly developed example of urbanization. He felt that studying New York would provide a glimpse of what was in store for Germany's urban life. As he put it, "After industrialization comes urbanization; but what comes after urbanization?" The only answer I could give him was this: "After urbanization comes death."

For if one looks at the modern American city—at New York City, for example—the conclusion seems inescapable that the city is a profoundly decadent society. Decadence does not particularly mean, here, moral decadence in the surface, conventional sense, although the city has plenty of corruption and vice and crime. Decadence means, rather, that state of perishing in which the city finds itself. The signs in the city—in every sector of its life—are signs of death, not signs of salvation. And it is precisely to this city which is perishing that the Church is called to minister.

Little can be said about the present estate of the churches in the city which does not sound as if the churches are ridiculous. Some churches, for example, have physically quit the city—closed down, sold out, and moved to the suburbs—only to find out that the same problem of the mission of the Church still plagues them, since the suburbs are satellites of the city and commuters spend much, if not most, of their time in the city.

Perhaps the churches which have remained physically in the city have eluded the Church's mission there more effectively—by virtually full-time preoccupation with ecclesiastical housekeeping, or by their massive indifference in practice to the excitement and conflict of the city, or by just plain malingering. Some churches have fled the city;

and those churches that have remained have, for the most part, been hiding out.

How well they have hid is illustrated by an incident a few years ago in one of the great cities. A new political administration had just been inducted into office in the state in which the city was located, and legislation was proposed which would modify the hours during which alcoholic beverages could be served on Sundays. The new governor of the state, sensing that some of the churches might be opposed to any liberalization of the law in this way, decided to write all of the leading ecclesiastical authorities and solicit their views on the pending legislation. The letter of the governor to the bishop of one diocese was in fact addressed in the name of the man who was bishop of that see twelve years previously and who had been dead for several years.

Consequently, the city pays little attention to the churches—save perhaps, on those patently absurd or innocuous occasions when the churches manage to call attention to themselves in such ways as calling a press conference to announce the discontinuance of pew rentals. If *that* is all the churches have to report to the city, it is probably shrewder to suppress the news, but that is just the sort of thing with which the churches are normally, albeit not yet exclusively, identified in the city.

The notorious fact is that the churches at present do not *know* the city. And yet the rudiment of the mission to the city is the immersion of the churches in the common life and the dispersion of Christians within the turmoil and travail of the city's existence. The rudiment of mission is knowledge of the city because the truth and grace of the Incarnation encompasses in God's care all that is the city. Mission in the city for the Church, and hence for Christians, means a radical intimacy with every corner and every echelon of the city's actual life in order to represent and honor God's concern for each fragment of the city.

THE CITY AND THE RECONSTITUTION OF FEUDALISM

The city, as it is today, emerges from the maturing of the industrial revolution. In North America and Western Europe, thereafter in the countries of the East, and even more recently in Latin America and Africa, feudalism is overthrown by industrialization, and industrialization is followed by urbanization. The city represents the realization of the forces and purposes unleashed in the industrial revolution. And the city is the fulfillment—if indeed there is to be such—of the promises of that revolution.

Those promises were that in the industrialization of production men would be set free from their bondage in work. No longer would a man be enslaved either to the land or to the landlord. No longer would a man toil only to maintain his own poverty and indebtedness. Now he might even share significantly in that which his labor produced. And if emancipated in his work, he would also become politically free—with time, opportunity, and the wherewithal for education for himself and for his children. That, in turn and in time, would mean that homage to heredity and class would be made obsolete. Then leisure and the arts would be for all, and men might even participate in their own government. The only limits upon a man, according to the ideology of the industrial revolution, were those indigenous to his own mentality, volition, health, competitive spirit, and luck.

Nowhere so far—unless it be, by some mockery, in the Soviet Union—have these promises been taken more solemnly, more literally, more religiously, and, ironically, more for granted than in the United States. Here they have been the propaganda line of the industrial and commercial powers, the core of the curriculum in public education, the pledges of every political campaign, and the moral theology of most American Protestants.

But look at the contemporary city to see what has happened to these promises:

1. Among the poor in the city, folk are still in bondage to the land and to the landlords. Unemployment is persistent, unemployability because of lack of urban occupational skills is common and increasing, and many of those who are employed can only find seasonal, marginal, menial jobs. Income is low and erratic, yet credit is easily available for necessities—groceries or furniture or clothes—though at premium prices for frequently inferior quality. The result is that people are encumbered by debts against uncertain future earnings. The speculators in slum real estate are generally absentee landlords, inaccessible to tenants except for the collection of the rents and profits of their holdings (sharp manipulation of slum property reaps as high as 25 to 30 per cent return for the investor).

23

Meanwhile, the economics of both public and private urban redevelopment have placed new housing beyond the means of the poor, apart from other sanctions like *de facto* segregation in housing in the city. Consequently, the poor of the city are immobile, bound to the places where they live, with little practical expectancy of moving out of the slums; in fact, almost the only mobility is the movement from one slum to another.

2. While the poor are confined to their ghettos, more and more space is being diverted in the city to luxury housing. In part the exodus of the middle classes contributes to this; it is also an accommodation to the interests of the utilities, builders, insurance companies, banks, some unions and universities, and other heavy investors in real estate. For principalities such as these it is more advantageous to redevelop the city for the rich than to rehabilitate it for the poor. Anyway, the chasm between the rich and the poor grows wider and wider, and the hostility between the rich and the poor, associated as it usually is with racism of one sort or another, becomes more intense and embittered.

3. But the poor are not the only city folk who are in subjection to the principalities that rule the city. The industrialization of production caused the inception of a new kind of work in which the product is, as it is cleverly called, services, rather than goods. The largest single element of the city's working, as distinguished from residential, population is an assortment of managers and middlemen, underwriters, factors, bureaucrats, brokers, bailors, lenders, promoters, consultants, attendants, and the like. Perhaps

these are more beholden, more manipulated, more expendable, more confined and conformed, more like serfs than the poor.

4. Meanwhile, the illusion is maintained and reiterated that public policy in the city in employment, housing, education, redevelopment, transportation, and the like is determined by the political administration elected by the voters. Therefore, public policy is supposedly oriented toward the welfare, safety, prosperity, and freedom of the person. But one does not have to live very long in the city to discern that the elected political administration exercises only a very modest discretion in questions of public policy. It is not just that politics is often corrupted by the personal aggrandizement of office-seekers and office-holders, but that the effective power to determine public policy is exercised by the great principalities—institutional powers: investment, commerce, industry, education, labor, and the like—and that policy as a result is oriented toward the profit and survival of these principalities.

In short, the modern American city which has emerged from industrialization and urbanization, especially the City of New York (for it is, after all, the prototype city), is not a place in which men have found freedom and society. This is no city of salvation. This is not where the promises of industrialization have been authenticated. On the contrary, this is a city in which the elemental spirit of feudalism still survives in spite of—perchance because of—technological and sociological and psychological change. The city is more a reversion to feudalism than an emancipation from it.

Medieval demons are not dead, for demons are indeed the ministers of death. They were not exorcised in the building of the city. They still exist there. The city is their present realm and their plunder.

THE REDUNDANCY OF THE CHURCHES IN THE CITY

I suggest that the promises of the industrial revolution have not been vindicated in the city and that they are exposed in the city as illusory. If the people have not been emancipated by industrialization and its aftermath, but are enslaved to the principalities and powers that rule the city in much the same manner as their predecessors in feudal society, then all this must be taken into account in the conception of and deployment of the mission of the Church to the city.

The Church must know what sort of place the city is, neither underweighing it, nor suppressing, blushing or flinching at, whatever *is*. But *that* puts the churches, particularly those of American Protestantism, in an anomalous and tender predicament. These churches are ill-disposed to undertake the mission to the city (else why would so many have sought to abandon the city?); they are unprepared to minister to the city because of diffidence toward and ignorance about it; they are reluctant to love the city, lest they risk their reputations and possessions. These churches are also immobilized from serving the city because they are still fascinated with the ideology and promises of the industrial revolution. Maybe the promises of the industrial era are fraudulent, but the Protestants still believe them, recite them, eulogize them, enshrine them, and chant them instead of the psalms.

While the Church of Rome has been and is still in some places the handmaiden of the ruling powers of feudalism, the churches of American Protestantism became and, to an awful extent, still are captivated by and captive to the ideological forces of industrialization. The Protestants in America theologized the ideas of the industrial revolution. They preached a radical and ascendant humanism in which some innate capacity of the individual to conquer, subdue, and rule the environment embellished the promise of industrialism that men would be free enough from work to have time for politics, education, and the arts. They thought that the revolution in the productive process and in the output of production rationalized a novel, albeit unbiblical, doctrine of work in which the dominion of men over the rest of creation was restored or imminently restorable and men would find not only adequate compensation, but personal satisfaction and moral justification in their daily work. They thought that the powers and principalities so evident and notorious in feudalism were deposed and destroyed in industrialization. So they just forgot about them, and, thereby, incidentally, served them handily.

The churches have been immobilized in the mission to the city on two counts: First they have not really wanted the gospel; they have, instead, abandoned it and replaced it with the ideology of the industrial revolution. Theirs is the very elementary heresy of ignoring the fall, denying the power of death, radically confusing the nature of sin, and supposing that men save themselves when they have the guts, positive will power, and, perhaps, a little luck. The irony of this, however, is that very few people in modern urban society really believe seriously any more the ideology of the industrial revolution, despite the nostalgic, ceremonial recognition still accorded it in the speeches of politicians, corporate executives, and commencement orators. The raw truth is that in practice no one living and working in the complex of contemporary mass society actually honors these ideas.

In other words, because they have become theologically incapacitated, the churches have pretty much forsaken the city both physically and psychologically. They do not know the city because they are stopped by a religion bearing only outer resemblance to the gospel; because they are not immersed in the common life of the city, their witness is peripheral, pietistic, self-serving, corny, and profane.

THE CITY AND SALVATION

It seems likely that if the churches were somehow rid of their beguilement with the promises of the industrial revolution and were to see the city as it really is, they would be seized with hysteria. So be it. Conversion is not always sudden or dramatic, but it is always traumatic.

The plea here is not just for the recovery in the churches of a biblical theology of work and for the restoration in the churches of a responsible theological understanding of the principalities and powers, though God knows both are needed if the churches are to return to and minister to the city. The plea here is for much more than that; it is for the renewal of the sacramental integrity of the churches. Mission to the city requires not just a renunciation of the fictional theology which now entraps the churches and their people, but the confession by the churches and the people of the churches that in and of themselves they are helpless to cope with the city or any bit of the city's existence.

Helpless, mind you, is not a synonym for hopeless; quite the contrary, the Christian hope becomes manifest in the very event in which a people or a man confess utter helplessness, for that confession *is* the first and free and most reckless acknowledgment of God's life and presence in the world.

Then the churches can again discern and rely upon God's presence anywhere in the world—even in the city. Then the celebrations at the altar of God's awful and fearsome, splendid and victorious presence in the world will be validated in mission to the city. Then the city will hear that it is God who builds the City of Salvation.

II. THE SCANDAL OF PALM SUNDAY

◇◇◇◇◇◇◇◇◇◇◇◇◇◇◇◇

**For because he himself has suffered
and been tempted, he is able to help
those who are tempted.**
Hebrews 2:18

◇◇◇◇◇◇◇◇◇◇◇◇◇◇◇◇

Men live in the city of death. All the cities and societies
of the world are places of death.

Men look to and serve first one and then some other
power of ideology and institution—on and on, over and
over again—in order to find the City of Salvation, but each
one turns out to be itself consigned to death, a witness to
death's power and reign. It is through these idols which
are themselves acolytes of death that death tempts men
with the hope of their own salvation. Death tempts men by
promising to save them from death; that is how cruel and
vain and filled with guile death is.

All images of the good society—all panaceas and utopias;
all idealisms and ideologies; all provisional hopes, compro-
mises, appeasements, corruptions, and failures in the life
of men in society in this world—are in the repertoire of
death's temptations. Plato's republic, Constantine's empire,
Rousseau's social contract, Jeffersonian democracy, Marx's

classless society, free enterprise, and world government are specific forms by which men are solicited, enticed, or coerced into the service of death. So, too, are the ancient Assyrian totalitarianism, the authoritarianism of the Caesars, the divine right of kings, colonial imperialism, the American Confederacy, nazism, Chinese communism, and all their legion counterparts. All such principalities in turn pay homage to death and are subject to it even as they promise men salvation.

God builds the City of Salvation. It is not some never-never land, some alabaster city beyond the realm of time, but a City, whatever be the final shape and reality of its fulfillment at the end of time, which has form and actuality here and now in the midst of this history. The City which God builds is a society which lives in this history in the midst of death, surrounded, as it were, by all the cities and societies of the world which are places of death. This City is free. For the foundation upon which God builds his City is his own freedom from and authority over the power of death—that is, the foundation is Jesus Christ.

In the event in which Christ is in this world alone on the Cross, when not only his enemies and the principalities of Israel and Rome, but also his friends, followers, and family have abandoned him to death, Christ is revealed as the embodiment, in his own person, of the City of Salvation. Christ on the Cross suffering the full indignity of death and enduring its final assault is beheld, then and there, as man reconciled with both God and the whole world. In Christ on the Cross God is forgiving the idolatries of men to the powers of death and freeing men from imprisonment in death. In Christ on the Cross is the reality embraced within his own person of the City of Salvation.

The City which God builds is not only for his own dwelling; it is for men and for the world in which all men and all things dwell with one another together with him. The City which God builds in Christ is the prophet and pioneer in history of the Kingdom which God covets for the whole of creation. And all those who believe in Christ as the personification of the City of Salvation are made members of his Body and elected citizens of that City on behalf of all those who, though they have beheld Christ, as all men have, yet persist in unbelief.

Many do not believe. Many men hate the Cross because it means a salvation not of their own choosing or making, but rather of God's grace and his mercy. Men hate the Cross because it means a salvation which is unearned, undeserved, unmerited. *Men would much prefer God to punish them than to forgive them because that would mean that God is dependent upon men and needed their obedience to be their God.* Then God would be in fact no different from an idol of race, nation, family, or whatever, and a man would feel justified either by his obedience to the idol or by the punishment of his disobedience.

Many do not believe, and so the Body of Christ has a task and mission to the world, not to add to the work of God in Christ, but to proclaim by the very presence of the Church and its members in the world the scope, design, and style of God's City of Salvation and welcome all into the same.

Many do not believe; and people of the Church are constantly tempted to return to unbelief. In the whole ministry of Christ, particularly among the events precedent to Holy Week, there is no more lucid instance of temptation than the fond interpretations given to Palm Sunday by the contemporary teachers and preachers of the churches. Palm Sunday is not a day of triumph, as it is so often depicted. Easter is the day of triumph.

Palm Sunday is a day of dramatic temptation for Christ. It is a day of profound frustration for the disciples and one on which the apprehensions about Christ on the part of the ruling authorities of Israel and Rome are exposed.

For Christians nowadays Palm Sunday is a symbol of the terrific confusion which burdens the Church as to the meaning and manner of the Christian witness in society. It is also a day which symbolizes the confusion about the constitution and life of the Church as the paradigm of society.

The scandal of Palm Sunday is the forerunner of the scandal which the churches to this day still suffer. One of its forms is the dismay, frustration, and opposition of those who call themselves the disciples of Christ when the *real scandal* of the gospel is confronted: when they are shown that Christ is exactly the One in whom and for whom all things were made, of whom the prophets spoke, whom the psalms praise, against whom death has no dominion, in whom all life is and is to be fulfilled, by whom the world is judged; when they are shown that Christ is just the One he is declared to be in the Word of God and which he confessed himself to be.

The substance of consternation is the desire for the gospel

to end in the political triumph of Palm Sunday. If the work of Christ would only end in *that* way, Christians would be spared the betrayal of Judas, the apathy and cowardice of the other disciples, the mystery of the Last Supper, and Gethsemane's sweat and agony. They would also avoid the accusations of the authorities and the ridicule of the crowd; the Cross and the descent into hell; the embarrassment for man in God's power in the resurrection; and the awful gift of Pentecost.

If only Palm Sunday were the outcome of Christ's ministry, Christians would be rid of the gospel and free from all that distinguishes them as Christians from the rest of the world. But the fulfillment of the gospel is not in the parade on Palm Sunday. What, then, does this celebration of Jesus by "the whole multitude of disciples" mean in the ministry of Christ himself and in the ministry of his Body, the Church, today?

THE TEMPTATION OF PALM SUNDAY

Palm Sunday, I suggest, represents in the ministry of Christ the same temptations with which he was confronted by the power of death during his forty days in the wilderness. The time of Christ in the wilderness was not at all a time of spiritual exercise or contemplation. To be in the wilderness is to be alone with the reality of one's own death, to be confronted with the reign of death in all the world. In the wilderness the power of death tempts Christ with the offer of worldly dominion, but Christ is victorious over all the claims and temptations of death. And death departs from him, as the account puts it, until an opportune time.

Palm Sunday is that opportune time for death to again tempt Christ with the offer of worldly power, though now death uses those who are Christ's own disciples to press the temptations upon him. After all their sacrifice and service to him, now the day was at hand when his Kingdom would be established. Had he not said so himself? The expectation of the disciples was that Christ would now become the king of an earthly realm; so they gather on that day to celebrate their new king.

But Christ is again victorious over the temptations of death. And so the gospel story does not end in the Palm Sunday parade. In the events which followed the multitude of the disciples quickly forsook Christ. For those who remained with him a few days longer, there must have been great bewilderment as they continued to protest and oppose his vocation. But before the week had passed Judas betrayed him, Peter denied him, and all the rest fled and hid.

Let us not be too harsh on these disciples, lest the same harshness be applied to us. The truth is that they really did not know who Christ is until after the resurrection, the post-resurrection appearances, and the ascension. Only at Pentecost did they realize that Christ had come not to establish an earthly reign, but to overpower the reign of death in the world—indeed, to reign over death in the world.

Think of the terrible frustration these disciples must have suffered in the days following Palm Sunday, when the opportunity for political success had seemed within grasp and yet Christ did not exploit it. Poor Judas, especially, is remembered with particular hardness nowadays, portrayed as he usually is as some monstrous traitor, a greedy, hapless, sullen, and despicable man. I suggest it is more faithful to the New Testament to see Judas as a man who had dedicated his life to a great cause and who on the night of the betrayal was desperately and pathetically disillusioned with the One who was his leader. Perhaps Judas felt that he had been betrayed by Christ. And why expect Peter to have the faith not to deny Christ? Only fools have courage for lost causes.

The rulers of Israel and Rome also saw Christ on Palm Sunday as what the disciples wanted and expected and besought him to be—a political leader. They were startled and apprehensive; therefore, they tried to stop the celebration lest Christ threaten or undermine their own power.

His family and friends and followers, on the one hand, and his enemies, on the other, failed on Palm Sunday to comprehend who Christ really is. All of them were captivated in the temptation with which the power of death confronts Christ. Palm Sunday is no day of triumph; for Christians it is a day of profound humiliation.

INVOLVEMENT NOT APATHY

Things have not changed much since then. The disciples of Christ today keep returning to Palm Sunday, possessed with nostalgia for the parade, beguiled by the temptation to achieve or imitate worldly power and to build an earthly kingdom.

Nowhere is this temptation more active and persistent than in the mission of the Church to the city. The historic error of foreign missions a half-century ago was in supposing that before the gospel could be heard, believed, and embraced by the indigenous people, those people would first have to be "westernized." The historic error of the so-called inner-city mission in recent years is in thinking that before the gospel can be heard, believed, and embraced by the indigenous people, they must first become middle class. Yet if the gospel is so contingent that it offers no comfort for a man, whatever his state or affliction, then it is no saving word for anybody.

But if Christians do not seek to build or to call into being an earthly kingdom in their witness in secular society, of what does their witness consist? Does the resistance and renunciation of temptation to political authority by Christ on Palm Sunday counsel Christians to withdraw from the political life of the world, ignore the common issues of secular society, or be indifferent to the turbulence and travail of the world?

No, there is no counsel of apathy in the Palm Sunday episode. Quite the contrary, it is the example of utter and radical involvement in the existence of the world, an involvement which does not retreat even in the face of the awful power of death.

The counsel of Palm Sunday is that Christians are free to enter into the depths of the world's existence with nothing to offer the world but their own lives. And this is to be taken literally. What the Christian has to give to the world is his very life. He is established in such an extreme freedom by the power of Christ, which is so much greater than the power of death, that the Christian lives secure from any threats which death may make.

It is in exercising this ultimate freedom in his involvement in the world that the Christian also understands how to use whatever else is at his disposal—money, status, technical abilities, professional training, or whatever else—as sacraments of the gift of his own life. The daily witness of the Christian in the world is essentially sacramental, rather than moralistic. The public witness of the Christian is a symbol and communication of his death in Christ every day in each situation in which he finds himself. He thereby demonstrates his faith in God's triumph over death in Christ. The ethics of witness to redemption are sacramental ethics of grace, rather than of prudence or of law.

THE ETHICS OF WITNESS

But such witness with respect to the world means involvement, not indifference; realism, not withdrawal; knowledge, not ignorance. The Christian is free enough both from his own death and from the reign of death in the world to realize and recognize the signs of death in that world: narcotics, slums, racism, unemployability, disease, or the oppression of men by the principalities of commerce, patriotism, sports, communications media, and ideologies. And the Christian is free to enter into the midst of all or any of these ordinary realities of the world's existence, knowing what they truly represent, without succumbing either to their lust for idolatry or the fear of the work of death of which they are evidence. The Christian is so empirically free from the threat of death in his own life and in the existence of the rest of the world that he can afford to place that life at the disposal of the world or of anybody in the world without asking or expecting anything whatever in return.

That is where the irony and confusion of so much of what is asserted to be Christian witness in society nowadays comes in. The mission to the city and specifically to the slums, the decrepit and depressed regions of the city, has been engineered by bodies, councils, committees, and commissions who neither individually nor corporately are seriously or radically involved, and certainly not to the point of risking possessions or reputations, much less death itself. Instead these ecclesiastical engineers ponder statistics of urban development, of the migration of races and nationalities, of the topography of the churches in the city; then they decide that a church building is needed here or a settlement house must be constructed there.

I am all for maximum use of whatever skills, techniques, data processes, or even gimmicks the social sciences can conceive and regulate, but none of them amount to much in terms of witness (though perhaps otherwise in terms of the image of the churches) unless there are in fact Christians on the actual scene day after day, day in and day out. First the Christians have to live a while in the streets before they can know how to minister to, how to *love*, the people of the streets and how to understand, to accept and enter into, the action on the streets. Because of his comprehension of the Incarnation—the entrance into and participation in human existence of God himself—the Christian must simply be there, no matter how unpleasant that may be.

Or, in other words, if I were a bishop in one of the great cities, I would not show my compassion for the trauma and violence of city life by building, financing, and consecrating any more church buildings or parish houses. Maybe some of those are needed, but first there has to be a depth and passion of involvement that, for the most part, there has not yet been. Only then can there be intelligent deployment of financial resources and shrewd location of physical facilities. If I were a bishop, I would first of all devote myself to walking the streets, trying to see the inner city for myself. I would, so to speak, make myself available to the actual inner life of the city; I would visit and try to listen to the voices that can be heard in the taverns and the tenements, on the street corners, and in the shops. First, I would try to hear the city, if, indeed, the city would tolerate my presence long enough to permit me to listen.

Then, I think, I would go out to scour the land to find perhaps five hundred Christians—men and women, clergy and laity—to commission and send into the city. When I had found and called these missionaries I would tell them that they were to go, probably in pairs, into the city and just live on whatever means of survival prevailed in the block or neighborhood to which they were sent; they would have to live, in so far as possible, as those to whom they were sent. I would instruct them that upon their arrival they should do only one thing: knock on every door. Most doors would not be opened, at least not readily. But when a door was opened, the missionaries would say: "We have come to be with you because God cares for your life, and, because God cares for your life, we also care for you." Period. There would be nothing more—no invitations to join the Church, no programs to offer for the people or their kids, no rummage to give away, no groups to join or meetings to attend, no gimmicks, no concealed motives, and no hidden agendas. There would be just the bare announcement of God's love and the freedom which that love gives people to love each other.

Of course, at first, because the world is so accustomed to guile on the part of those who come in God's name, this message would not be either welcomed or believed. But with persistence, some would receive the message. Then there would be time enough to deal with all of the other issues of Christian witness beyond the event of merely caring, such as whether some should be baptized or join a congregation, whether a new congregation should be called into being, whether any particular facilities were appropriate to the witness in this place, and so on. But first of all, the Christians (the Church) must simply be in the world, sharing in and caring eloquently and honestly for the life of the ordinary world—or the life of any man— just as it is.

There may be those, I am aware, who will think that such tactics of witness as these are fanciful. The answer to them is, on one hand, the relative absence of any other serious witness in the city at the present time, despite all the charts and blueprints and building funds, and, on the other hand, the fact, again and again illuminated in the

42

ministry of Christ himself, that the witness of the Christian in a place is his very presence in that place.

The witness of mere presence means that the witness of Christians is characteristically a secret, an event unknown except to those who are themselves involved in the situation. The real witness of Palm Sunday is not the parade or what the disciples or the secular authorities saw; it is the encounter between Christ and the power of death. The real witness on Palm Sunday is hidden in these other events. And so it is for Christians today. The witness is secret, except to those actually involved and except when the Christian people gather openly and publicly as a society to offer to God their involvements jointly and severally in the world's existence. It is then, so to speak, that all that represents their secret witnessing while dispersed in the world is encompassed in their worship; and it becomes the specific content of their confession, praise, and thanksgiving for the manifold presence of God in the world. In that way the secret witness is shared throughout the Church, and thus it becomes public.

In seeing the gathered congregation the world has a glimpse of the Kingdom of Christ. This is the only apparent image of the community reconciled with God in which the members are also reconciled to themselves, to each other, to all men, and to all of creation. The worshiping congregation is the only evidence of the Christian society's existence in the world, and it is the exemplification of that which the world is called to be and of that which is vouchsafed by the ministry of Christ. No ambition or attainment of political, economic, or moral power by the Church can substitute for the worshiping community as a portrait of the Kingdom. On the contrary, the worldly pretensions of the Church tend mainly to bewilder the world and to hinder its recognition of the true society living already in this world in Christ.

A RADICAL LIFE

This style of life, this ethics of witness, means that the essential and consistent task of Christians is to expose the transcience of death's power in the world. That is a task which will not be exhausted until God's mercy brings this history to an end and fulfillment on the Last Day. Thus, the Christian in secular society is always in the position of a radical—not in the conventional political sense of that word, but in the sense that nothing which is achieved in secular life can ever satisfy the insight which the Christian is given as to what the true consummation of life in society is. The Christian always complains of the *status quo,* whatever that happens to be; he always seeks more than that which satisfies even the best ideals of other men. Or, to put it differently, the Christian knows that no change, reform, or accomplishment of secular society can modify, threaten, or diminish the active reign of death in the world. Only Christ can do that, and now his reign is acknowledged and enjoyed in the society which bears his name and has the task of proclamation in all the world for the sake of that part of the world still consigned to the power of death.

At the same time the witness of Christians in the world

is always both repentant and penitential. It is repentant in
that Christians acknowledge the fallenness of life and the
reality of sin and then confess—as much in and through
their action in the world as in their worship—their own
sins: shortcomings, omissions, failings, infidelities, profan-
ities, weaknesses, vanities, angers, indulgences, errors, and
corruptions. By intercession (as representatives before God,
in behalf of and in the place of other men) they also confess the sins of the world, in which they share, and which
they call upon other men to confess for themselves. This
confession and intercession is repentance. But it is also
penitential: recognition and realization of sorrow, regret,
remorse, grief, mourning, and contrition for the offense of
their own sins and the sins of others against God's own
person and to his creation.

The penitential act, the authentication of true repentance,
which invariably follows repentance and is the sacramental
expression of repentance, is not an act of recrimination by
which a man indulges in judging and punishing himself.
Nor is it some form of restitution as if what has been done
could be undone or as if there could be a return to the
situation prior to the sin. Both recrimination and restitution
are ways in which men attempt, even after acknowledging
their sins specifically, to justify themselves by allaying God's
judgment or earning his forgiveness. Such tactics may work
between a child and a parent, between a criminal and society, or in the moralistic and legalistic religions, but they
have nothing to do with the event of repentance and the
penitential act characteristic of Christian witness in action
and worship in the world.

What is involved in penitence, in its sacramental sense, is not making some sacrifice to amend, blot out, or absolve former sins. It is a passionate, prayerful, and fearful appeal to God's mercy in the sacrifice of God in Christ for the sins of the world. Thus true repentance and the penitence that ensues from it is always at once acknowledgment of the state of sin in which all men live, confession of specific sins known and unknown, and confession of faith in God's forgiveness. And this is, all the while, not only an action of Christians for their own sakes, but one of the concrete forms of the service of Christians for the world. It is inherent in the witness of Christians and of the Church in the world.

Characteristically, too, the Christian witness is attentive to those who live on the extremities of society—to the outcast and the unpopular, to those who are least in society. The concern of the Christian for the one who is least is a way of representing his concern for everyone. The outcasts include, of course, the poor, the sick, the prisoners, and those socially discriminated against. But for some man the outcast may be his own wife, or child, or business colleague, one who is not particularly destitute in the usual ways. Whoever the outcast is in given circumstances, the Christian is free enough from his own self-interest, from the necessities of preserving his own life, to intercede for another and to take up the other's self-interest as over against the rest of the world. Finally, of course, to care for the outcast means to love your own enemy.

Because I was associated as an attorney in the cases of the Episcopal clergy arrested during their Prayer Pilgrimage in Jackson, Mississippi, I have been asked by many fellow churchmen to defend the action of these clergy against complaints that they were stirring up trouble, or that they should not have left their parishes to go on the pilgrimage, or similar stereotypes. It is possible to defend the pilgrimage in terms of the impact it has had in the general civil rights crisis, especially in the South, in relation to the Freedom Rider cases. But the most cogent defense, as if any were really needed, is that these Christians found a ministry to the very ones who had arrested them and who were keeping them in jail. That ministry was to their very own enemies. And so it is for Christians that they love even those who revile them.

If this is the way Christians live, if such are the ethics of witness, if this is your style of life, the world will think you an idiot for trusting God more than men or idols. And you will be tempted. But remember on the day of temptation, which is always *today*, that Palm Sunday is not a day of triumph, but a day of shame. Easter is the day of triumph. And, when you are tempted, look then to him who suffered and was tempted, for he is able to help those who are tempted.

III. CHRIST AND THE POWERS OF DEATH

◇◇◇◇◇◇◇◇◇◇◇◇◇◇◇

Now in putting everything in subjection to man, he left nothing out of his control. As it is, we do not yet see everything in subjection to him. But we see Jesus, who for a little while was made lower than the angels, crowned with glory and honor because of the suffering of death, so that by the grace of God he might taste death for everyone.

Hebrews 2:8b-9

◇◇◇◇◇◇◇◇◇◇◇◇◇◇◇

Christ defeats the temptations of worldly power with which death confronts him on Palm Sunday; and in the days immediately following he is delivered to death by one of his disciples, condemned to death by the ruling authorities of the nations of Israel and Rome, and abandoned to death by the rest of his disciples.

Christ is neither delivered nor abandoned by his disciples into the hands of just some evil, envious, or frightened men: he is given over, and he surrenders, to Israel and Rome. And in the encounter of Christ with these powers there is exposed the relationship between Christ and all principalities and powers. The ecclesiastical and civil rulers who accuse, try, condemn, and execute Christ act not essentially for themselves as individuals, but as representatives—indeed, as servants—of the principalities. It is, of course, in the name of these powers that Christ is put on trial. He is accused of subverting and undermining the nation, of threatening the nation's existence, survival, and destiny.

That *this* is the accusation should, by the way, dispose of the legend, so popular in modern treatments of the trial of Christ both in Good Friday sermons and popular secular versions of the event, that Christ is innocent of any offense and tried and condemned because of some corruption or failure or miscarriage of justice. Of the charge against him, Christ is guilty beyond any doubt.

In any case, the significant aspect of the trial is that it is not just an encounter between Christ and some men who were his enemies. The most decisive clash in all history is this one between Christ and the principalities and powers of this world, represented by and symbolized in Israel and Rome.

The understanding of principalities and powers is lost nowadays in the churches, though, I observe, not so much so outside the churches. About a year ago, for example, I was invited to lecture at the Business School of Harvard University; earlier on the same day, I also met informally with some students at the Divinity School. Since graduates of the Business School live their professional lives and work so obviously within the spheres of dominance of great corporate and commercial principalities, I decided to speak there about the meaning of the principalities. Though the Business School students were not especially theologically sophisticated, and certainly none had been theologically trained, they displayed an awareness, intelligence, and insight with respect to what principalities are and what are the issues between principalities and human beings. Yet, when the same matters had been discussed earlier with the divinity students, I found that most of them felt that such terms as "principalities and powers," "ruling authorities," "demons," "world rulers of the present darkness," "angelic powers," and the like—terms so frequently used in the Bible—were archaic imagery having no reference to contemporary realities.

It appears, in other words, to be widely believed in the churches in the United States that the history of redemption is encompassed merely in the saga of relationships between God and men. What there is of contemporary Protestant moral theology typically ignores any attempt to account for, identify, explicate, and relate the self to the principalities, although empirically the principalities seem to have an aggressive, in fact possessive, ascendancy in American life. Because the biblical references to principalities and angelic powers are so prominent, and because the powers themselves enjoy such dominance in everyday life, their meaning and significance cannot be left unexamined.

What are principalities and powers? What is their significance in the creation and in the fall? What is their relationship to human sin? How are these powers related to the presence and power of death in history? What is the meaning of the confrontation between Christ and the principalities? Does a Christian have any freedom from their dominion? There can be no serious, realistic, or biblical

51

comprehension of the witness of the Church in the world unless such questions as these are raised and pondered.

WHAT ARE PRINCIPALITIES?

There is nothing particularly mysterious, superstitious, or imaginary about principalities, despite the contemporary failure to discuss them theologically. The realities to which the biblical terms "principalities and powers" refer are quite familiar to modern society, though they may be called by different names. What the Bible calls "principalities and powers" are called in contemporary language "ideologies," "institutions," and "images."

A principality, whatever its particular form and variety, is a living reality, distinguishable from human and other organic life. It is not made or instituted by men, but, as with men and all creation, made by God for his own pleasure.

In the biblical understanding of creation, the principalities or angelic powers, together with all other forms of life, are given by God into the dominion of men and are means through which men rejoice in the gift of life by acknowledging and honoring God, who gives life to all men and to the whole of creation. The dominion of men over the rest of creation, including the angelic powers, means the engagement of men in the worship of God as the true, realized, and fulfilled human life and, at the same time and as part of the same event, the commitment by men of all things within their dominion to the very same worship of God, to the very same actualization of true life for all things. All men, all angels, and all things in creation have origination, integrity, and wholeness of life in the worship of God.

Just as men differ in their capacities in one sense or another, just as there are varieties in human life, so also there are varieties of principalities which can be distinguished one from another, though they all retain certain common characteristics. Let us consider various examples of principalities.

PRINCIPALITIES AS IMAGES

One kind of principality is designated by the word *image*. An obvious example of this sort is the image that comes to be associated with some celebrity and bears the same name as the celebrity. Thus, there was for a time the movie star named Marilyn Monroe. The person is now dead, but the image "Marilyn Monroe" is by no means dead. Not only have certain memories either personal or public survived the death of this person, but the name survives; the name, in fact, attaches to a reality which was given new life when the person of that name died. The image called "Marilyn Monroe" did not die but went on to a new and, some would say, more vigorous life. In point of fact, then, Marilyn Monroe is not dead because there were two lives that claimed and used that name: one a principality, the other a person; only the latter died, the former is, if anything, livelier than ever.

All the talk of Marilyn Monroe as the great American "sex goddess" or as "the symbol of youth" is not just the prose of Hollywood journalists, whether they realize it or not. Marilyn Monroe, whoever she was as a person, was and is a genuine idol, an entity, bearing the same name and likeness as the person, with an existence, character, and power quite distinguishable from the person who bore the name.

An image is a very common variety of angelic power, though often of much less dignity and influence in the world than other kinds of principalities. In fact, every person is accompanied in his life by an image; he is often controlled or destroyed by his image, and invariably it survives him. The images associated with persons in public life—movie stars, politicians, and the like—are perhaps more easily identified than those which accompany a person relatively unknown to the public. Thus, James Dean, another young movie star who died violently some years ago, with whom apparently multitudes of adolescents identified themselves, was survived by an image which has been the subject of extreme adulation for years. Or, take Franklin Roosevelt: the man is dead, but the image of Roosevelt still lives and still exerts a profound influence not only on American politics and policy but upon the lives of many other nations and peoples.

Once in a while the public image of a person becomes much more than just an idol, becomes a principality of such magnitude that the image is comparable to an institutional or ideological principality. Adolf Hitler, for instance, whoever was the person by that name, became and is to this day such a principality. And in terms of the relationship between Hitler the person and Hitler the principality, it may well be that long before his actual suicide the person named Hitler had been wholly obliterated by the principality named Hitler; that the person had indeed been possessed by a demon of that name; and that the devastation and massacre wrought in the name of Hitler was not the work of just some dark genius of the man, nor even of the man's insanity or gross criminality, but of the awesome demonic power that possessed him.

In any case, the form of principality identifiable as the public image bearing the name of a person exists independently of that person (though the person may be wholly dependent upon the principality). The form is distinguishable from the person, lies beyond his control, and is in conflict with the person until the person surrenders his life in one fashion or another to the principality. The principality requires not only recognition and adulation as an idol from movie fans or voters or the public but also demands that the person of the same name give up his life as a person to the service and homage of the image. And when that surrender is made, the person in fact dies, though not yet physically. For at that point he is literally possessed by his own image. The demand, then, made in the conflict between the principality and the personality is one in which the whole life of the person is surrendered to the principality and is given over to the worship of the image.

PRINCIPALITIES AS INSTITUTIONS

The institutional principalities also make claims upon men for idolatrous commitment in that the moral principle which governs any institution—a great corporation, a government agency, an ecclesiastical organization, a union, utility, or university—is its own survival. Everything else must finally be sacrificed to the cause of preserving the institution, and it is demanded of everyone who lives within its sphere of influence—officers, executives, employees, members, customers, and students—that they commit themselves to the service of that end, the survival of the institution.

This relentless demand of the institutional power is often presented in benign forms to a person under the guise that the bondage to the institution benefits the person in some way, but that does not make the demand any less dehumanizing. I recall, for example, the situation of a law school classmate of mine. When he was graduated he accepted a position with one of the great Wall Street law firms, an institutional power in its own right, though engaged in serving some of the great corporate principalities. During the summer, before he began work at the firm, he married. He did not consult or inform his superiors in the firm about his marriage prior to the event. Later, when he reported for work and the firm learned that he was now married, he was told that he should have consulted the employer before marrying, but, since he was married, it would be advisable for him and his wife to refrain from having any children for at least two or three years. Furthermore, for the sake of his advancement in the firm, he should and would want to devote all of his time both in the office and in his ostensibly personal life to the service of the firm, and children might interfere with this. In the end, the claim for service which an institution makes upon a man is an invitation to surrender his life in order that the institution be preserved and prosper. It is an invitation to bondage.

PRINCIPALITIES AS IDEOLOGIES

Ideology is perhaps the most self-evident principality in the world at the present time. Communism, fascism, racism, nationalism: all these are principalities and powers. Humanism, capitalism, democracy, rationalism—though Americans think of these as benevolent powers—are also principalities and share all the essential characteristics of those ideologies to which America's enemies are committed.

Communism—or, more precisely, Marxism as distinguished from Leninism, Stalinism, or post-Stalin Soviet communism—is a particularly lucid illustration of the nature of an ideological principality. Marxism asserts that it reveals and upholds the secret of history, that the destiny (literally, salvation) of all men and all nations is to be found and fulfilled in the ascendancy and dominion of Marxism in the world. It claims sovereignty over all history, and the moral significance of any man's life (or, for that matter, the existence of any institution or nation) is determined in relation to the power and prosperity of the Marxist ideology. This ideology therefore requires of men, institutions, and nations an unequivocal and militant obeisance, a sacrifice of all other supposedly lesser causes and rights to the idol of Marxism.

Other totalitarian ideologies have, of course, represented

the same sort of example of the principalities and powers which Marxism today represents. But do not suppose that the ideology of American society, though more diffuse and less systematic and theoretical than Marxism or the other totalitarian ideologies, is any different in its essential characteristics as a principality. Americans are now constantly, incessantly, and somewhat vehemently assailed with the word that the ultimate moral significance of their individual lives is embodied in and depends upon the mere survival of the American nation and its "way of life." There seems, to me at least, less and less of a public consensus about the content and style of that American way of life, just as there is an obviously increasingly intense controversy within the Communist world as to what the Marxist way of life is and is to be. But that only means that the survival of the nation as such becomes the idol, the chief object of loyalty, service, and idolatry. Or, to put it a bit differently, the historic ideological realities in American history, those of capitalism and democracy, are now perhaps displaced by elementary nationalism. But in any case the pre-eminent factor in terms of which, it is claimed, men will find their own justification is in service to the nation, in the offering of all other things for the sake of national survival. Or, in the inaugural words of President Kennedy: "Ask not what your country can do for you; ask what you can do for your country."

It should be recognized that in describing the principalities and powers in terms of the realities which are nowadays called images, institutions, or ideologies no attempt is intended to sharply distinguish the varieties of principalities. Frequently, one will have characteristics of the others. Though according to these descriptions the principality bearing Hitler's name would be called an image, this was, as has been pointed out, a principality which had the attributes of ideological and institutional principalities. The same sort of thing is true of other principalities. For example, every nation is a principality, but it would be ridiculous to identify a nation as just an institutional power, although it is that clearly when one considers it in the sense of the governmental structures in a society. At the same time, the nation is associated with ideological powers and partakes of the nature of them—the American nation with the ideological elements of democracy and capitalism, the Soviet nation with the ideological forces called communism, some of the new nations of Africa and Asia with the ideologies of nationalism, and so on. Sometimes, too, the principality of the nation is, as it were, personified in the image of a ruler. Thus in France, DeGaulle *is*, as he himself seems fond of mentioning, France. And that is not only embodied in the constitutional institutions of the French nation, but in the image of DeGaulle himself.

THE CONFLICT AMONG THE PRINCIPALITIES

Many other principalities and variations thereof which are familiar in the world today could be identified and named. Money is such a power. Such folk heroes of the country as George Washington, Jefferson Davis, and Abraham Lincoln are principalities. Sex, fashion, and sports are all among the angelic powers. The image of motherhood or that which Philip Wylie calls "momism" is one of the powers. In England, the institution of the Crown is a principality. Patriotism is such a power. Religion, as distinguished from the Christian faith, is a principality. Men are encompassed in their ordinary daily lives by a great constellation of principalities.

The present consideration of what the principalities mean in modern terms is, intentionally, quite rudimentary, seeking only to show that when the Bible speaks of principalities reference is made to such realities as images, institutions, and ideologies. These existed not just long ago but also exist today.

For any man today, surrounded as all men are by such a great array and variety of principalities, there is the experience of living and working under the simultaneous and conflicting claims of many powers. Each principality claims a man's loyalty, service, and worship; each makes essentially the same demands that a man regard it as his god, as the one in the idolatry of which a man's life will gain moral significance. Each makes the same claim, but a man is beset by the several claims of the principalities of class, race, nation, profession, and family; all made more or less at the same time and each insistent upon taking precedence over everything else.

But this bewildering and intensely complex array of principalities exists in the world not only in conflict with the lives of men. The principalities exist in acute conflict with one another in their competition, as it were, for the loyalties and services of men. The principalities are not just common enemies of human life; they are enemies of each other and, as such, engaged in deadly warfare among themselves.

The intensity and acute complexity of the conflict among the principalities is shown, in recent history, in the denunciation of the "personality cult" in the Soviet Union. Stalin, whoever he once had been as a person, had, like Hitler, become possessed by his own image, and his image took upon itself the attributes of the principalities of ideology and institution. This was recognized in the world as Stalinism, as a principality distinguishable from the other principalities which claimed identification with the cause of world communism. While Stalin lived, the principality bearing his name apparently dominated virtually every aspect of the life of the Soviet government and people, as well as the apparatus of the Communist party in the Soviet Union and throughout the world.

But upon the death of Stalin, the great struggle for authority to rule the Soviet nation and the Communist parties began or, at least, broke into the open. It was not just a conflict among men, among the Communist politicians who survived Stalin's death. It was a momentous clash between the principality named Stalinism and the ideological principality identified with the regime of Khrushchev. From all reports, within the Soviet Union and the Communist parties still dominated by the Soviet Union, Stalinism was defeated in this conflict, although it may be that the struggle still continues within the later ideological war between the Soviet Union and Red China. Much too little information and insight into this situation is available to ordinary people in America or elsewhere. Therefore, we cannot understand the conflict between these great principalities at work in the Communist world. The significant point is that, while all principalities are arrayed against men, they are also locked in ferocious combat with one another and such conflict among the principalities has enormous repercussions for the practical lives of men.

THE MEANING OF DEMONIC

Like all men and all things, the angelic powers and principalities are fallen and are become demonic powers. "Demonic" does not mean evil; the word refers rather to death, to fallenness. An angelic power in its fallen estate is called a demonic power, because it is a principality existing in the present age in a state of alienation from God, cut off from the life originating in his life, separated from its own true life and, thus, being in a state of death. In the fall, every man, every principality, every thing exists in a condition of estrangement from his or its own life, as well as from the lives of all other men, powers, and things. In the fall, the whole of creation is consigned to death.

The separation from life, the bondage to death, the alienation from God which the fall designates is not simply to be accounted for by human sin. The fall is not just the estate in which men reject God and exalt themselves, as if men were like God. The term does not merely mean the pretensions of human pride. It is all that and something more. The fall is also the awareness of men of their estrangement from God, themselves, each other, and all things, and their pathetic search for God or some substitute for God within and outside themselves and each other in the principalities

62

and in the rest of creation. So men, in their fallenness, are found sometimes idolizing themselves, sometimes idolizing snakes, bugs, other creatures, or natural phenomena, or sometimes idolizing nation, ideology, race, or one of the other principalities. It is to such as these that men look to justify their existence, to find and define the lost meaning of their lives, and to fill the place of God himself.

The search is pathetic because it is futile. The principalities are themselves consigned to death just as much as the men who worship them. Thus, the idolatry of the demonic powers by men turns out always to be a worship of death.

To put it another way, that dominion which men receive from God over the rest of creation (including their dominion over the principalities) is lost to them in the fall and, as it were, reversed, so that now the principalities exercise dominion over men and claim in their own names and for themselves idolatrous worship from men. Men do not create the principalities nor do men control them; on the contrary, men exist in this world in bondage to the principalities. No man escapes enduring the claims for allegiance and service of the principalities. For a man to live in the state of fallenness is to endure these very claims.

Whatever other distinctions may be made among the various principalities, remember that they are themselves fallen and demonic; the substance of the claim for idolatry which all principalities assert against men is the same. Concretely, each principality boasts that men will find the meaning and fulfillment of human life in service to the principality and to that which abets its survival; a profound concern for self-survival is the governing morality of every principality. This comes first. To this all other interests must be sacrificed; from this all else, including an individual's life and work, takes its significance; by this is a man judged.

The principalities claim, in other words, sovereignty over human life and history. Therefore, they not only compete and conflict with one another for the possession and domination of the lives of men, but they also deny and denounce the sovereignty of God. But do not let the arrogance of the idols conceal this fact: when a principality claims moral pre-eminence in history or over a man's life it represents an aspiration for salvation from death and a hope that service to the idol will give existence a meaning somehow transcending death.

PRINCIPALITIES AS POWERS OF DEATH

Apart from the sovereignty of God which the principalities challenge and reject, the yearning for freedom from death and the quest for the restoration of true life represented therein are rendered ridiculous by the evident grandeur of the presence and power of death in this world. Death is greater than any of the principalities and powers, and none of them prevail against it. The whole of creation exists under the reign of death. Men die. Images, though they survive men for a time, also die. Institutions and ideologies, though they have immense survival capabilities, eventually die. Nations die. The reality which survives them all is death itself. Death, it seems, is the decisive, ultimate and dominant truth in history. No man is safe from his own death who looks for his salvation in idolatry of some principality, whatever it may be.

The consignment of the principalities themselves to death means that they hold no saving power either for themselves or for men. The principalities are themselves acolytes of death in this world, and man's idolatry of them is really the concrete form of his bondage to death.

Men, nowadays at least, appear generally reluctant to admit the presence and power of death in the world, despite the signs of death's presence and activity with which they are everywhere encompassed. Part of that reluctance is the notion that death is merely the terminal experience of this life, that the meaning of death is contained in the final agony when a man expires, and that death is the event of biological extinction. Death is all that, but its meaning is hardly exhausted in the actual event of physical death, and the reality of death's work in the world is not sufficiently explained by giving attention only to the last moment.

A man begins to die when he is born. Death accompanies him in every event and experience of his life in this world; it constantly overshadows all that a man says and does; and it is the final outcome of his labor. Though a man amass great wealth or many possessions they will neither protect him from death nor themselves be free from death. Though a man project his own life in his offspring, the offspring also die. Though a man make himself an amiable reputation by his thoughts or words or deeds, the memory of him dies as certainly as he himself does. Posterity is no more an effective denial of death than the superstitions of Christian Science or the fantasies of Greek mythology.

A man's death begins in his birth, but before then death has been at work in this world, just as it will continue to be after a man's body is buried. The scope of death's presence and vitality is from the first day to the very last day, from the beginning of time to the end of time. In this world, men and all the principalities and all other things exist within the realm of death.

It is probably not so difficult, nor perhaps so traumatic, for those who live outside of the amenities and privilege of American middle- and upper-class society to acknowledge the presence and activity of death in the world. Nor does one have to leave America and see, as I have seen, the gas chambers of Auschwitz, the slums of Glasgow, the lepers begging in Bombay, or the poverty of Port-au-Prince to discern the signs of death's presence. Go only to Woodlawn in South Chicago, to the Negro settlement in Magnolia, Mississippi, or north of 96th Street into East Harlem in New York. There you will see death at work in the crumbling, decrepit tenements holding and housing six or eight times more people than can be accommodated by available space, light, air, heat, or plumbing. There is the evidence of death's activity: in the breeding of disease in the filth of cellars and gutters, in the attacks of rats upon babies and children, in the tension and violence of the streets, in the cynicism and fraud of the politicians and business people who prosper like parasites from the preservation of poverty. Those who are poor or otherwise outcast in American society, like their brothers in India or Haiti or wherever, cannot mistake the presence of death because it is the reality they have seen every day, everywhere around them in the most immediate and specific forms.

But remember that death has many faces. It is quite as much present and active in the communities less afflicted by unemployment, poverty, disease, hunger, and the like. I recall, for instance, visiting a small midwestern town a few years ago in order to be the best man at the wedding of a friend of mine. It was one of those places in which virtually everybody in town, apart from a few shopkeepers and a few Negroes who worked as domestic help, was employed in the management of a great industrial corporation. For the most part, everyone lived in a comfortable and spacious house, belonged to the country club, attended some church, worked for the same company, did and thought and said the same things, and acted the same way.

The home in which I stayed was one in which a young college graduate, a junior executive in the company, and his wife were my hosts. They had been married for four or five years, approximately the same length of time for which the husband had been working for the firm. They had no children because, as they explained one evening, it seemed better to them to be free to participate fully in the social and business (the two were, of course, inseparable in such a place) life of the community, thereby promoting the husband's career, much like my law school classmate with the Wall Street firm. Their modern, convenient, well-equipped, heavily mortgaged, conventional, middle-class household was empty as a home.

During the same visit I attended seven parties in a day and a half in honor of the bride and groom. I am not loath to go to parties, but it did strike me that in this case it was being a bit overdone, especially since the guest lists at each of the parties were literally identical. The guests would all just go home to change their clothes between parties. At the one on the morning of the wedding I turned to another guest and said, "I've only been here since yesterday, and this is the seventh party I've been to." The other guest replied, "Oh, that's nothing; since the first of the month (it was then the 17th of the month) I have been to thirty-three parties here!" How deadly, I thought to myself, can life be when one spends so much of it with the same people doing and saying the same things in the same places.

Before my visit to this barren place ended, I learned some other things about the lives of the people there: the two early-middle-aged married couples who had recently exchanged partners; the suicide, a couple of months before my visit, of a prominent and presumably promising junior executive; the experiments "for kicks" of the town's adolescents with narcotics; and the alcoholism of one of the local clergy.

There was too little life and joy in this place. Death was indeed, as far as I could discern, very much at work there despite the security of the people from the ordinary threats of disease, poverty, or overcrowding. Death works just as well through affluence, social conformity, boredom, lust, and ambition.

The signs of death's reality and ubiquity are read, in other words, in every place, in all that happens. Death is not only the terminal experience; it is the imminent truth about every and any event in this world. Death is a living power in this world, greater, apart from God himself, than any other reality in existence. Death is no idea or abstraction or mere destination, but the pervasive power which apparently overrules everyone and everything else in the whole of creation.

Not so very long ago, the presence and power of death were recognized and acknowledged by men as the devil. Nowadays people, both within and outside the churches, are hesitant to identify the reality and activity of death in terms of the descriptions and portraits of the devil regarded by their ancestors as significant and comprehensible. But that should not hinder modern folk from ascertaining the objective existence in this world of the power of death. One does not have to believe in an anthropomorphic idea of a devil with horns and a tail and a red complexion to admit, understand, and reconcile with any other realities of contemporary life the vitality of the power of death in history.

One does not have to be a literalist about the classical images of the devil to observe, realize, and seriously regard the truth that in this fallen world as men know it in their ordinary lives, in this world with all of its principalities and powers, the ascendant reality, apart from the reality of God himself, is death. Except for God's own intervention in this history in Christ, it is the power of death which reigns in the world, in all things, at all times, whether recognized or not by men or nations. That power reigns not just eventually, but immediately; not just ultimately, but imminently; not just now and then, but all the time; not just in certain places, but everywhere; not just some day, but every day; not just for a few, but for all men; not just for human life, but for all of life.

Though the clash between Christ and the principalities in his trial and execution is the decisive and normative encounter, it is not at all the only occasion in the historic ministry of Christ when he is confronted by the principalities. The final showdown is again and again foreshadowed in Christ's life on earth.

The apprehension with which he is regarded by the worldly authorities during the Palm Sunday celebration and during Holy Week is first exposed in the consternation and rage with which Herod received the news of Christ's coming into the world. At the same time, remember that it is part of the authentic miracle of Christmas that those who gathered at the stable to adore him do so as representatives of the whole of creation, as emissaries of all men and all creatures and all things. Those who come to worship and honor Christ in his birth include the Magi who come as ambassadors of the principalities of the world. For a moment, as it were, in the Christmas event the sovereignty of Christ over all the world is revealed, and it is in that event that the world has a glimpse of the very restoration of creation from the fall, a foretaste of the world become the Kingdom of God.

The Lordship of Christ is disclosed in the adoration in the Christmas miracle, but the hysteria and hostility of Herod

70

at Christ's coming into the world foreshadows the later encounters between Christ and the principalities. The time of Christ's temptation in the wilderness as a particularly significant episode has already been mentioned. But, in addition to that, Christ confronts the principalities when he stills the tempest, heals the sick, frees the demoniac, upsets the traditions of Israel by eating with sinners, or shows that he is Lord of the Sabbath. And, Christ's wilderness temptation is repeated in Palm Sunday. Yet that is not the last encounter between Christ and the principalities, for he goes to cleanse the Temple, and Lazarus is raised from death. Then, betrayed and forsaken to death by his disciples, condemned to death by the rulers and crucified and buried, he descends into hell—into the event in which the presence and power of death is most militant, pervasive, ruthless, and undisguised.

In some of the episodes, as in the wilderness, the crucifixion, and the descent into hell, death openly confronts Christ; in others, Christ is visited by one or another of the principalities as emissaries of death. In all of these encounters, the principalities represent the awesome and manifold powers of death.

The victor in each specific encounter is Christ. That is important because it means that the power of Christ over death is not merely a transcendence of death as the terminal experience or as biological extinction. Thinking of the resurrection as having reference only to the crucifixion and entombment of Christ (the terminal event of his earthly life) underlies the wistful, vain, and false ideas about the immortality of the soul or life after death which so violate the gospel and corrupt the minds of many church people. Each specific confrontation between Christ and death and between Christ and one of the principalities as one of the powers of death foreshadows the resurrection, exposes and heralds the overwhelming authority over death which Christ has and holds from the beginning of time to the end of time. And the resurrection encompasses and represents all of these particular historic encounters in a single, consummate, and indeed cosmic disclosure of the triumph of Christ over death.

The resurrection is impregnated with all that has gone before; these encounters of Christ with death and its powers in history mean that his triumph over death there shown is offered for men and for the whole world. His victory is not for himself, but for us. His power over death is effective, not just at the terminal point of a man's life, but throughout his life, during *this* life in *this* world, right now. This power is effective in the times and places in the daily lives of men when they are so gravely and relentlessly assailed by the claims of principalities for an idolatry which, in spite of all disguises, really surrenders to death as the reigning presence in the world. His resurrection means the possibility of living in this life, in the very midst of death's works, safe and free from death.

But what of all of these notions and speculations about a life after dying, after the day of the undertaker? The Christian, the man living by the authority of and in the freedom of the resurrection, is saved from fond and wishful thinking about that. The Christian has no anxiety about his disposition after his life in this world: in fact, he knows little or nothing about the matter; but he knows all that he needs to know, which is that the reality and truth of the resurrection has been in the present life so radically verified and realized that he is confident and joyful in leaving himself in the judgment and mercy of God, in all things, forever and ever.

Christ's resurrection is for men and for the whole of creation, including the principalities of this world. Through the encounters between Christ and the principalities and between Christ and death, the power of death is exhausted. The reign of death and, within that, the pretensions to sovereignty over history of the principalities, is brought to an end in Christ's resurrection. He bears the fullness of their hostility toward him; he submits to their condemnation; he accepts their committal of himself to death, and in his resurrection he ends their power and the power they represent. Yet the end of the claims of the principalities to sovereignty is also the way in which these very claims are fulfilled in Christ himself. The claim of a nation, ideology, or other principality to rule history, though phony and futile, is at the same time an aspiration for salvation, a longing for the reality which does indeed rule history. In the same event in which the pretension of the principality is exposed and undone, how and in whom salvation is wrought is disclosed and demonstrated. In Christ the false lords of history, the principalities, are shown to be false; at the same time, in Christ the true Lord of history is made known. In Christ is both the end and fulfillment for all principalities, for all men, and for all things.

IV. THE RESURRECTION AND THE CHURCH

Pentecost is the event marking the constitution of the Church in the world. In Pentecost the Church as the Body, and Christians as members of Christ's Body, are authorized and empowered by God to live in this world, free from bondage to death and free from idolatry of the powers of death. In Pentecost the fruits of the ministry of Christ, the triumph of the resurrection itself, are bestowed upon the Church and those, then and thereafter, baptized into it.

This is an awful freedom into which the Church is born and into which the Christian is baptized. It is a freedom to live in this present age, during the remaining time of death's apparent reign, without escaping or hiding or withdrawing from the full reality of death's presence, bearing the brunt of its powers, yet jubilantly confident at the same time of Christ's victory over death and all the powers of death. It is the freedom to live anywhere, any day, in such a way as to expose and confound the works of death and at the same time to declare and honor the work of Christ. It is the extraordinary freedom "to be *in* but not *of* this world," as the language of tradition puts it: it is the freedom to be in a world which appears to belong to death and which death claims but in fact to belong to Christ.

It is not a freedom given to the Church or to the baptized, for the sake of either, as if to covet their own safety from death. That was the stumbling block for the Hebrews both before the resurrection and later in the course of the controversy in the Church about the mission to the Gentiles; and it remains a stumbling block, let it be noted, in contemporary churches. Nor is this freedom given to the Church and to the members of Christ's Body for God's sake, as if it were a gesture he needs to make; or for the sake of the members that certain men may have wholeness and completeness of life. Rather, it is given in order that the world and all therein may recover wholeness and completion of life.

The Body of Christ receives this freedom for the sake of the rest of this world which still suffers the bondage and agony of death. This freedom that is given to the Church by God is no act of necessity, but one of generosity; and his generosity is not acknowledged and affirmed unless the Church and the baptized people, having had their lives returned to them from death, are now generous with their lives in and for the sake of the world, and that without measure. In other words, only where the gift of this freedom is received with the dignity with which it is given by God, and so used and exercised, is there obedience to God and witness to his grace, truth, and power in the resurrection. Living in the freedom of the resurrection is, for the Christian and for the Church of Christ, the ethics of obedience.

THE RESURRECTION AND THE CHURCH

THE CHURCH, THE CHURCHES
AND THE PRINCIPALITIES

Although the Church and the baptized people are called to and given this freedom in obedience in Christ, they are nonetheless assailed incessantly by the claims and conflicts of the principalities and powers of this world.

In the United States—though this is no uniquely American problem—the principalities of race, class, and status would hold captive the Church (or, more precisely, the churches in their present divisions) in the service of the causes of these principalities in order to preserve, entrench, and extend one or another of them. Indeed, the demands to serve such principalities, and the accommodations made in the name of the Church to these demands, are among the reasons in America for the division of the Church into a multitude of denominations. Denominationalism, in so far as it originates in sectional, class, racial, or similar interests, both renounces the freedom of the gospel and is an instance of servility to the principalities and powers.

THE CHURCHES AND RACISM

To no principality—unless it be to those of commerce and finance, which are often allied with and committed to racism —have the American churches been more notoriously and scandalously and complacently accommodating than to the principality of racism.

Racial discrimination and segregation, though often in

ingenious guises, still mars the lives of most congregations of most denominations. And this condition persists even in the face of the significant political and legal changes taking place in the nation in the relations of the races.

These congregations that condone or practice segregation and discrimination represent not just an open defiance of what has at last become a public policy favoring integration in public and quasi-public life—transportation, education, housing, employment, and most public accommodations— and not just a failure to treat conscientiously the meaning of baptism as the sacrament of the unity of all people in Christ. They also represent a surrender to the principality of racism and to its claim that its survival and continuance is of such importance as to take precedence over both the law of the land and the integrity of the Church as Church. Let us not suppose for a moment that it is only some of the predominantly white denominations that give themselves over to racial segregation; some Negro denominations do exactly the same. And, above all, let us not think that surrender to the principality, the demonic power, of racism is an issue only for congregations in the South; it is as much an issue in congregations in the North, although in a more subtle and less vulgar form.

Do not assume, either, that the churches and people of the churches who have entered the service of racism all suffer from obstinance, ignorance, hatred, or pathological disorder. Many church people, church groups, and churches with the most benign intentions and socially liberal impulses are also accomplices to the idolization of racism. For example, if one examines the pronouncements of preachers

and church assemblies over the past thirty years (before
that, there was silence about race in the churches in America,
unless one goes back to the Reconstruction period and to
the Abolitionist movement before and during the Civil War)
it is difficult to locate a coherent, theologically substantive,
or authentically prophetic statement about the relations
among the races either in society or in the churches. What
can be found aplenty are empty promises, theological super-
ficialities, and pietistic indifference. What can be found,
usually, are recitations of the most elementary humanistic
propositions about equality and liberty. And while these
premises of humanism are influential ideas in the ethos of
the American nation, they come nowhere near embodying
or expressing the concern of the gospel for the races and
sorts and conditions of men, nowhere near representing and
upholding the character of the Church as the community in
history in which the unity of all men in God and in the
worship of God is already manifest. Insofar as the churches
in America, in other words, have in practice followed society
in the evolution, now become revolution, in race relations
and have simply imitated or repeated the slogans of humanism, they have forsaken or suppressed the unique word
which they exist to proclaim, to serve, and to be. And they
become by default—by silence, indifference, and irrelevance
—handmaidens of the principality of racism, for the principality of racism is as well served by appeasement as by
idolatry.

Within the last year there has stirred among the churches
and the church hierarchy a sudden realization, a frightful
consternation, that humanistic and pietistic benedictions en-

treating "better race relations" were not and are not sufficient to contain or mitigate the Negro revolt. It dawned at
last upon at least some of the American churches that an
insurrection had begun, that the cause of "good race relations" had turned into a desperate and bitter racial crisis.
The dawn came at about the same time for the President,
too, and for the commercial and journalistic and educational
powers of the white establishment in America. Emergency
meetings at the highest ecclesiastical echelons were summoned. Church budgets were loosened to provide funds in
both indirect and direct support of the civil rights movement. Clergy were now authorized to participate in dem-
onstrations and other forms of direct action. Red tape was
out. The ecclesiastical authorities and common churchfolk
began asking, many for the first time, "what do the Negroes
want?" and began calculating what concessions might be
offered to the insurrectionists (not realizing that the question
"what do they want?" is no generosity but, in fact, contains
the seed of white supremacy; the very question assumes
that the white man, in the churches or in society, remains
and should remain in control, in the role of deciding and
ruling). In brief, the sudden excitement in the churches and
within the leadership of the churches over the racial crisis
seems to arise from an anxiety over the survival of white
ascendancy in the churches and in the leadership of the
churches rather than from either compassion for the people
of color or passion for the gospel which is the means by
which all people may dwell in reconciliation.

I have with my own ears heard more than one ecclesiastical leader of a predominantly white denomination admit

that the very recent concern of the leaders of these churches in the racial crisis is a recognition of the fact that integration in American public institutions is now imminently inevitable. Therefore, it is important for the churches to intervene swiftly enough so that when the day of certain victory of the Negro revolt comes the churches will be found to be on "the right side," which means, if such comments are taken at face value, on the side that is going to win.

This last minute involvement of the churches and their leaders in the racial crisis seems to be mainly motivated by fear, but that does not necessarily vitiate it. This involvement can be for some churches and church people in America— and one may hope that it will be, despite what prompts it— a means of seeing how racism in any of its manifestations divides the Church, how it is in fact one of the powers of death at work in the world, and how it can only really be met in the freedom from death with which Christ has set men free.

The point here is not to question the sincere motivation of any leader or church now finally involved in direct action in the racial crisis; their own words and actions will speak for them. The point *is* to emphasize how deeply and terribly the American churches are compromised in many instances and places to the principalities which rule American society, especially those of race and class and status. The complexity of the implication of the churches with the causes of the principalities is very great. A congregation or denominational board, for example, may not indulge in praise or other open service to the principality of racism; but it may nonetheless be beholden to that principality by virtue of the fact that

81

the capital assets of the congregation or board are invested in commercial, industrial, or real estate enterprises that profit from and support racism in one form or another.

Any honorable and effective attempt on the part of the churches to free themselves of complicity with racism is bound to involve them also in a rigorous and selfless scrutiny of their commitments to, and vested interest in, the principalities of finance and commerce in order to find out whether and how far their investments represent a *de facto* service of racism. As a matter of fact, some churches and boards have, in the recent past, examined their investment portfolios with this issue in mind. And a few have exerted pressure on enterprises in which they hold substantial investments for policy changes in the hiring of Negroes, advertising, and the like. But most have not yet done this. One major denominational body, after considering such action, decided that it was inappropriate for a church body to employ economic pressure as a tactic, despite the massive evidence that such pressure has been the single most effective weapon in the integration struggle. One trustee on this particular board put it this way: "The responsibility of the trustees is to invest the funds of the church to make money."

Undoing the complicity of the churches with racism will also lead, as we have previously observed, to agonizing reappraisal of other issues and commitments. The same churches and church people will have to confront their fondness for the ideology of the industrial revolution, and for those which have become shrines of this form of secularism there will indeed be traumatic readjustment.

THE RESURRECTION AND THE CHURCH

THE CHURCHES AND THE NATION

What is at the heart of the relationship between the churches and the principalities is an overlooking of the fact that, at any given period in history, the principalities are those incumbent institutions and ideological forces which rule, or feign would rule, the world or some sector of society.

The claim to homage that the principalities assert against men and, in their conflicts, against one another, they assert as well against Christians, against churchly institutions, and, indeed, against the Church of Christ as such—just as they repeatedly did against Christ himself. That is, the principalities need and solicit and demand in terms of obligation that the Church abet their survival as principalities; as the incumbent ruling powers in the world, they claim and require support by the Church of that *status quo* most profitable and congenial to the enhancement, preservation, and prolongation of their ruling power. Thus, in another day, the principality of absolute and hereditary monarchy needed, sought, demanded, and received the commitment of the ecclesiastical authorities to the doctrine of the divine right of kings. At another period the churches, in the name of mission, became too much the agencies of Western European and, later, American colonialism and industrial society. In the United States, the churches, along with the institutions of home, family and, sometimes, school, have been aligned with the "American way of life." Often, it seems, they have been its so-called bulwark.

But of all the principalities—whether of class, race, commerce, ideology, or whatever—none in America or in other countries is more persevering and grandiose in its demands upon the Church than the nation. The essential claim with which the principality of the nation addresses the Church in America is, simply, that the Church stand ready to serve the national self-interest at any given time, however that interest may be defined. The claim is not merely asserted against the Church, but it is also backed by formidable sanctions; that is, there is the implicit threat that if the Church does not subscribe to, dignify, and give precedence in all things to the national survival, then the Church's own existence will be threatened or curtailed, persecuted or suppressed.

In Rome, at one time, the sanctions were imprisonment, torture, and casting of the Christians into the arena with beasts. In Nazi Germany, not so long ago, the sanctions were exile, execution, and concentration camps. In modern Britain, the sanctions may be loss of property interests, of status at the royal court, or the diminishment, at least, of one's ceremonial role in the Establishment. In Franco Spain, the sanctions are exclusion from the educational process, persecution of religious dissenters, and supervision and censorship of social morality. In the United States, the sanctions are loss of tax exemption, of nominal but equal recognition for all faiths in public events, or, in different circumstances, the encouragement of a multiplicity of sects and denominations. The sanctions vary, significantly; but all are directed toward securing the commitment of the Church or the several churches to the survival and self-interest of the nation.

One way, in America, in which the churches have accom-

84

modated themselves to the nation is by their acquiescence to the very popular notion that religion is supposed to have only to do with "religion," not with the great issues of public life, with anything controversial, or with any cause that might call into question, disrupt, or change the *status quo*. Very often this conception of the private and separate nature of religion is invoked to shut the mouths of the clergy, by asserting that they are supposed simply to preach, not talk about politics or other matters about which they allegedly know nothing.

Impetus, of course, is given to this isolation of religion from public life by the misconceptions commonly held about the constitutional separation of church and state, although any serious study of First Amendment cases will show that there was no intention of implying separation of religion from society, or of muzzling the Church to prevent its speaking out on social issues. In any case, the principality of the nation is served by the silence of the Church on issues confronting society; the nation willingly tolerates a silent, uncritical, uninterfering Church concerned only with such esoteric things of religion as public worship.

In some instances, however, the Church is still permitted to intervene in public life in this country, so long as it intervenes on the side that protects the nation and the stated public policy. As a practical matter the churches in America have become accustomed to entering the public arena in order to bolster the national unity and solidarity, in order to serve the interest and survival of the principality of the nation. But it is only with increasing infrequency that they will risk addressing any serious, critical stand on nationally significant issues. As we have seen, there has been a dearth of radical witness or prophetic utterance among the mainline churches on the racial issue. On that issue, up to the present moment, the churches have generally followed and endorsed prevailing public policy, whether earlier that of segregation or *de facto* segregation, or currently that of integration.

Apart from a tiny minority of pacifists and a few other individuals, to cite another instance, the churches have been pathetically servile to the nation on the issues of war and peace. In World War II, in the Korean conflict, and in the debate about the morality of nuclear war (admitting, of course, significant individual exceptions) the churches and church people for the most part dutifully blessed the cause of the nation with a dignity of allegiance that ought to be given only to God.

In short, where the churches have not just been silent and preoccupied in practicing religion for its own sake, they give evidence of having lost any critical relationship to or any substantial independence from the principality of the nation. One recalls the controversy which still smolders over a study document published by the National Council of Churches a few years ago concerning the relations of the United States and Red China. The statement was *not* an official stand of the Council or of any of its constitutional governing bodies, but a *study* document, drawn by a group of foreign policy experts, inviting public discussion of the impasse in U.S.-Chinese relations. It did not advocate any precipitous, drastic, or immediate changes in the nation's China policy, but it did challenge the cloture of public debate on China policy which then prevailed and still prevails in this country. That study document was and continues to be grossly distorted and misrepresented by an assortment of radical right-wing factions and persons, both within and outside the churches, who exploited it as an example of the churches' meddling in politics and of the churches' hostility to the national interest.

The attacks on the Council have been made not only by sectarian extremists who used the document as ammunition for their almost hysterical opposition to the Council and the ecumenical movement and by political extremists who are intent on preserving forever, apparently, the rigidity of Sino-American relations, but also by many moderate, respectable, if not very well informed, church people who are sincerely convinced that, contrary to the gospel, the churches should stay out of controversy. The hullabaloo which was precipitated by this mere study document illustrates how far the churches have become suffocated in addressing the nation in any terms which might be interpreted as critical of prevailing national policy. And it is a fairly safe prediction that, having suffered such blatant misrepresentation in this matter, the Council will not be bold enough now or in the future to speak critically about other national issues.

In this nation the churches, I suggest, have little more, if any, public freedom to address the nation in the name of the gospel than have the churches in East Germany where, as here, they are still permitted to hold services and the like and to enter the public forum so long as they do so to support and apologize for the nation. Part of the reason for this is a confusion in the churches themselves between the public freedom of the churches prescribed by the nation and the freedom which the Church is given in the gospel. In the United States, the churches live in a society which constitutionally professes the freedom of public worship and, in a formal sense, the public practice of religion. It increasingly appears, however, that the only use of that freedom which is socially approved and sanctioned by the nation is confined to the mere formalities of religious observance: that is, to the use of religion, religious institutions, and religious authorities in order to rationalize, serve, and sanctify the national self-interest. Accordingly, the jargon and images of religion are used for the preservation and even aggrandizement of the principality of the nation.

The issue then under these circumstances, whether in America, East Germany, or any other nation, is how the Church (and the churches) can maintain and exercise the freedom of the gospel to proclaim and serve the gospel, which the churches are constantly tempted to forswear in order to protect the public freedom of the churches as religious institutions in society. On one hand, the Church cannot be the Church unless it exercises the freedom of the gospel in which it was constituted at Pentecost. But shall the Church exercise this freedom in such a way as to provoke the nation to take away the freedom of the churches to exist as religious institutions? Can the Church, at times, stand over against the nation and oppose what the nation defines and determines to be its self-interest? Can the Church counsel its people or itself to engage in disobedience to prevailing public policy? And if so, what is to be said of the New Testament admonition of St. Paul and others about Christians subjecting themselves to the ruling authorities? In a word, can a Christian engage in civil disobedience?

THE CHURCH VS. THE NATION

There is a sense in which the Church as Church, by its very constitution and nature, always stands over against the nation and all other principalities and powers in this world. But the actual tactics of the witness of the Church in, to, or against the nation and world may vary widely. The tactics in particular situations may differ, but the essential witness, whatever the tactics, remains the same. Civil disobedience is not the only tactic open to the Church in its witness. But since it is a very radical one, it symbolizes as well or better than others which might be discussed the essential difference between the freedom of the gospel given to the Church in Pentecost and the public freedom accorded the Church and churchly institutions by the nation.

Historically, civil disobedience has been a venerable and persistent issue in Church-nation relations. Christ himself was accused of "subverting the law" of Israel. Herod feared Christ as one threatening to undermine his temporal power. Pilate examined Christ to determine whether he was a political enemy of Rome and hostile to the rule of Rome. And then there followed the numerous other tensions and collisions between Christians and the nation. St. Stephen, the Apostle Peter, St. Paul, and the era of the Catacombs are all in that chronicle. Even after Constantine had established a political entente between the Church and state, and

Thomas Aquinas had attempted a theological *rapproche-ment* between the gospel and secular law, the history of conflict between Christians and the nation continued.

All the Reformation theologians were also forced to deal with the issue. It was a critical one in the United States when Christian abolitionists were smuggling slaves out of the South. It is a continuing concern among pacifists who are Christians. The issue is raised today by those within the Church who are restive in East Germany and Berlin, like Bishop Otto Dibelius, or, in South Africa, like Archbishop William Ambrose Reeves. It is a present and urgent question now in this country in so far as Christians and the churches become actively implicated in the racial crisis.

At the same time, however, let it not be forgotten that civil disobedience is not exclusively a Christian tactic. From time to time many others have resorted to some form of it. In this country, the most frequent recourse to civil disobedience has probably been in tax, traffic, liquor, and gambling cases; this means that *very few* people have been innocent of using some form of civil disobedience. In the present racial crisis, civil disobedience takes on the sophistication of the final means, short of open insurrection, of resolving this issue if, indeed, it is to be resolved. Both integrationists and segregationists countenance and practice civil disobedience, it ought to be noted, although it has usually been only the segregationists (the most extreme ones at that) who counseled violent civil disobedience.

The classical argument—as distinguished from the biblical reason—to which Christians have resorted in the question of their obedience to the nation and their subjection to the ruling authorities, is the claim that the insight and experience of the Christian community gives Christians (or the Church) a special knowledge of the will of God. Whenever the law, policy, or self-interest of the nation notoriously conflicts with this understanding of God's will, it is insisted, the higher determination of the will of God must prevail, even if this means the open opposition in the form of civil disobedience to the decrees and self-interest of the nation.

This is a popular and recurring doctrine, and it admittedly has the appeal of simplicity. But it treats too casually the fact that the Church's very existence is a witness over against the nation even when the tactics of witness do not take so drastic a form as civil disobedience.

The peril in this traditional reasoning lies in the confidence with which it assumes that any particular group of men in or outside the Church know with certitude the will of God. This "will of God" turns out invariably to serve, protect, or sanction the self-interest of those who are so confidently informed of what God's particular will is.

The superficiality and temptation of this approach to the issue was illustrated in the New Orleans parochial school desegregation issue, in which *both* sides declared that they knew and represented the will of God in the specific instance. One recalls too, among many other illustrations that might be given, that at a time when Britain and America and the other allies were assuring themselves of God's preference for their cause in World War II, some Nazi philosophers were giving the same assurances to the German nation.

The service that Christians and the churches owe to the nation which is consistent with the freedom of the Church in the gospel must be understood in somewhat different terms, I suggest. The Church knows that in the very freedom in the gospel any nation regardless of distinctions and characteristics is a principality, a demonic power, a fallen reality consigned to death, one of the powers of death. The Church recognizes that the nation, as such, demands that it be idolized by its citizens and by other principalities. But the Church also acknowledges the nation as representing one of the realities of creation—God's gift of life in society, life in which all things in creation have their true existence, under and within the dominion of men, in the service and worship of God. The Church remembers this, despite the brokenness of all relationships among all men, all principalities, and all things in the fall, and anticipates and expects the restoration of this for the whole of creation.

Hence the Church *vis a vis* the nation is always in the position of standing against the nation in the nation's bondage to death; at the same time, the Church is always in the position of standing for the nation in a most profound way that recalls the vocation of the nation in the service of God. The Church's fundamental service to the nation is its recognition of the reality of that nation as the structure of the common life of the true society.

No nation is that as yet; no nation will become that this side of the very end of history. But the Church exists to remind all nations of that which, in the mind of God in creation, they are and of that which, by the grace of God in the Eschaton, they are again to be.

So when the Church in its manifold witness in, to, and against the nation recognizes the authority of the nation to make, enforce, administer, and adjudicate public policy and law, to govern the life of society, the Church is doing so not to lend credence to the pretensions of the nation as an idol, a fallen principality. On the contrary, the Church thus exposes precisely those pretensions and so affirms the real vocation and life of the nation. In this sense, then, the Christians know that the nation holds and exercises its function and office under God (that is, as a gift from God, even though the gift is denigrated by the service which the nation now offers to death) and that this is held under the terrible scrutiny of God's judgment.

The Church reminds the nation, as it does any other principality, of the origin of its life, of the service which it owes to God, and of the accountability of the nation to God in ruling the common life of men in society. The Church, in other words, honors and submits to the authority of the nation in a way which calls upon the nation to honor God, in whom all authority originally, essentially, and finally resides.

This means the relationship between the Church or the members of the Church and the nation is *never* one of uncritical allegiance or obedience. This means, concretely, that the Church can never accede to any demand of the nation that the nation itself become the idol of men's worship. That demand is made nowadays not only in the so-called totalitarian states, but also, more and more openly, in so-called democratic states like the United States. And if by thus exposing the idolatrous claims of the nation, the Church suffers the loss of any public freedom for its institutional life, then so be it. The survival of the Church does not depend upon such favors from the nation, but rather upon its obedience to the truth of the resurrection, which is the freedom given to the Church by God and which no principality may destroy, diminish, or take away.

Whenever a situation arises in which the Church stands over against the nation, or where it resorts to civil disobedience, it is important to understand that Christians do not engage in civil disobedience as anarchists. Christians do not believe in civil disobedience for its own sake, although they may resort to it from time to time as one of the tactics of witness *vis a vis* the nation. They engage in civil disobedience not in order to overthrow the rule of law and the authority of the nation, but to affirm the true vocation of the nation. They do so not merely as a means of changing public policy, but as a means of reminding the nation of its transience and ultimate impotence and of assuring it, even in the midst of its most grandiose pretensions to sovereignty over history, that only God is God. But wherever the Church and the Christians take recourse to civil disobedience they willingly, readily, and freely bear whatever are the consequences of that disobedience.

The Church, in that way, takes upon herself the nation's hostility toward God, accepts the condemnation of the nation, and is persecuted, suppressed, dispossessed. When church members are imprisoned, executed, or exiled, they accept these as a means of upholding the vocation of the nation, namely, to exercise its authority in civil life as a service to God. Thus, even in circumstances which evoke civil disobedience, the Church is subject to the nation, while using the freedom that God has bestowed upon the Church in the resurrection.

CHURCH AS PRINCIPALITY

Sometimes the Church dishonors the freedom which God has given it by supposing that the public freedom which the nation accords the institutional existence of the Church is essential to the proclamation of the gospel and its service and witness in the world. Sometimes the Church yields or gravely imperils its integrity as the Church by becoming the handmaiden of the ruling principalities of race, class, or commerce. At other times the Church becomes so preoccupied with the maintenance and preservation of its own institutional life that it too becomes a principality. Within American Protestantism, where the Church is radically divided into sects and denominations, this last situation is most acute and apparent.

When churches are principalities they bear the marks essential and familiar to all other principalities of an institutional and ideological character. The moral principle which governs their internal life, like that which governs a corporation or university, is the survival of the institution. To this primary consideration, all else must be sacrificed or compromised.

Churches and church bodies may be principalities in a variety of forms. A single congregation or parish may be a principality. Or a great denominational headquarters may be one. The tradition of a given church, in much the same way as in society, may rule as a principality. The image of a church leader or ecclesiastical authority may be a principality. Committees, commissions, and councils that burgeon into vast bureaucracies may be principalities. In all these situations the churchly principality invites the world to serve its own preservation and prosperity, seeks and needs the service of men for its own survival, and, indeed, demands that men regard it as an idol.

The demonic character of a churchly principality cannot be hidden by the simple retention of some of the condiments of the Christian faith. Thus, much of what is now discussed and practiced in the American churches as the witness of the Church does not really pertain to the witness of the Church to the life and action of God in the world, but rather to the witness of the Church to itself as churchly institution. And while there may be a legitimate witness to the Church as Christ's Body, service to the institution is not synonymous with it and certainly not synonymous with witness to the Word of God.

In some times and places, the churchly institutions make extravagant demands of homage and service both upon men and other principalities. For example, in some societies, including some regions of this country where a particular sect or denomination has achieved such political and economic power that it dominates the government, the state may be required to defend its property, safety, and even its doctrines. Apart from such local exceptions, however, the churchly principalities do not have that much dignity *vis a vis* other principalities, although they still exist and can be identified in American life.

Such churchly principalities stifle and suppress Christians who resist putting the institutional self-interest before their freedom in the gospel. One might cite dozens of specific cases of this. I mention only one here to illustrate the problem, because I know at first hand the extraordinary measures that were taken to conceal what happened. The incident involved a clergyman who had worked for some years, mainly in the Deep South of which he was a native, in the racial crisis. This Christian minister recognized that more was involved theologically and confessionally in the racial crisis than recitations of humanistic ethics and assurances of good intentions, or programs of study about "race relations" and the annual observances of Race Relations Sunday. He therefore used his access to white Southerners to preach the gospel, to go among his native people as an evangelist and apologist. He understood that as a man has his own life renewed in the life of Christ he is set free to love himself and *all* men. He knew that the reconciliation wrought by Christ encompasses the only real reconciliation there can be among those of different races. As he saw it, the racial crisis had more to do with the meaning of Christ for men than all of these programs and pronouncements and conferences and committees. He thought that race also had something to do with the renewal of the Church.

But it came to pass that he was summoned by his superiors and colleagues within the churchly institution and told that he had become a great embarrassment to the institution because some people were beginning to think that the institution had no "positive program" in "race relations";

and, besides, the institution could not afford to have a man on its staff who was just going here and there preaching the gospel. There had to be a "positive program"; in other words, the priority in the man's work had to be that which would gain recognition for the institution, enhance its prestige, and prove that it was doing something. Homage to the churchly principality had to come before esteem for the gospel.

One of the serious issues for laity when confronted with the claims of such a churchly principality for homage and service is that the laity who do enter into such service are dissipated in it and are thereby diverted from their witness to and against the principalities of commerce and politics to which they are exposed in their daily life and work. They are dissipated not because the struggle against a churchly principality is any different as witness than that against any other principality, but because they will find no courage for the struggle if all that they know or are involved in, in the name of the Church, is some churchly principality.

It is worth repeating that to discern that there are churchly principalities such as these mentioned does not in itself reflect upon the sincerity or motives of any person related to such institutions. Rather, it is to recognize that this is, after all, a fallen world, and church institutions are not exempt from the fall, though there be another sense in which the Church is free from the bondage to death which characterizes the fall. It is important to note also that on the part of many who are privy to the churchly principalities there is a certain naïveté about their personal capability to change and reform the institution. Indeed, the void in Protestant moral theology in accounting for and treating the principalities and powers is nowhere better illustrated than in situations where the notion continues to prevail among church bureaucrats that they control the institution; whereas, in truth, the principality claims them as slaves.

This does not mean that Christians should be loath to work in churchly institutions, but it does mean that those who do should be aware of the reality which confronts them and should not be romantic about it because the principality bears the name "church." Above all, they should be prepared to stomach the conflict which will surely accompany their use of the freedom from idolatry of even churchly principalities which Christ himself has secured.

THE HOLY NATION

The truth and power which the Church invokes and upon which it wholly relies in confronting, combating, and refuting the principalities as powers of death, is none other and no less than the gift of the Holy Spirit, by which the Church was called into being and in which it was first constituted. Unhappily, for the contemporary churches and for the edification of their people, the Holy Spirit has been assigned to the most peripheral and ethereal regions of Christian teaching, preaching, and practice. No name by which the presence and power of God in this world is called, in the Christian faith, is more frequently intoned than that of the Holy Spirit, and yet no name is more carelessly uttered, vaguely understood, or frivolously used. The name of the Holy Spirit is too often invoked in prayers and preaching and churchly deliberations without either clergy or laity really seriously comprehending what the name actually identifies, designates, and means.

The Holy Spirit denotes the living, acting presence and power of the Word of God in the history of this world: the presence and power which lives and acts now in unity and integrity with the works of the Word of God in creation, redemption, and judgment, as well as in solidarity and identification with the advent, birth, ministry, death, descent, resurrection, and Lordship of Jesus Christ in this world.

In plain language, the Holy Spirit is the power and presence of God's Word seen and heard in this world. It is wholly consistent with and integral to the action of the Word of God in creating the world, sustaining its existence, in giving life to all men and to all things. It is the same presence and power which is authenticated by the revelation of the Word of God in the personhood of Jesus Christ.

So much is this creation and all that lives within it the work of the Word of God, that in all life, in all men, and in all things the Word of God indwells. The Holy Spirit refers to the Word of God as that Word is hidden in every facet, aspect, event, person, and thing in the life of this world. In Jesus Christ, this indwelling of God's Word by his mercy in his own creation which is named the Holy Spirit is exposed for all to behold not only as the promise and hope of salvation but as the unique, decisive, and universal accomplishment of salvation.

Christ is possessed, in the whole drama of the work of

God in him, of the Holy Spirit, of the power and presence of the Word of God in this world which God made for himself. The conclusive, consummate, and indeed cosmic revelation of that is the resurrection. But then, to show that revelation to the world which does not yet believe in the resurrection, Christ, as it were, shares the Holy Spirit with the disciples at Pentecost, and in that event they become possessed also of the Holy Spirit. And thus, then and there, the Church as Christ's Body is born. That birth is at once the birth of the Church as such and the birth or rebirth of each member of the Body, of each disciple, and by the authority of that event men are thereafter baptized into the same Body.

The Church is born and lives (no matter what the state of churchly institutions may be at any given time, as the Orthodox Christians lovingly remind other Christians) in the gift of Pentecost, and men (though they be sinners or unfaithful) are baptized in the same gift. This is so and remains so until the very end of time, until God's judgment is known to all men and in all creation in the perfection of his mercy. This is so not because men are good or pleasing to God, much less to one another, or because anyone deserves or earns his salvation, or because a person is faithful, least of all because a man upholds traditional or even true theological convictions, or because the churchly institutions are incorruptible or uncorrupted, or because, in the name of the Church, apostasy or heresy is occasionally opposed and routed. It is so not for any of these reasons, but solely because of the honor with which God regards himself—

his unsurpassing love for and unsurpassed fidelity to himself and all of his creation. What saves the world is God's exuberance in his own handiwork.

Christ shares the gift of Pentecost, and the Church is born in that sharing of the Holy Spirit.

It is Christ, possessed of the Holy Spirit, who is triumphant in all his encounters with the powers of death, with all the principalities, and, indeed, with the presence of death itself. And it is this, concretely, which is the gift which the Risen Christ shares in Pentecost with the Church. The gift of the Holy Spirit is, then, authority and victory over death and over every power of death.

Specifically, that gift, that freedom, lies in the power given to the Church by the service of Christ to discern and identify, and then to expose and exorcise, the powers of death, whatever form they may take, however they may be disguised, whenever they insinuate themselves against the Church, or put forth their false claim to dominate the life of the world or of anybody in it.

The Church, notice, does not, independently of God, have, hold, or exercise any strength against the principalities. God, as the world has been shown in Christ, reserves to himself this awesome prerogative. But the Church, in the gratuity of Pentecost, is enabled to witness to God's authority over the principalities in his victory over death by its knowledge of death, its discernment of the powers of death, and by unveiling and laying bare the works of death in this world.

How, then, is the Church to go about identifying and exposing, discerning and exorcising, the powers of death? The

Church does so by being the Church, just as a Christian does the work and witness of a Christian by simply being a Christian—as awful and as simple as that may sound.

To put it more bluntly, in Pentecost the Church is born into a freedom from death. This is a freedom to be used in this world, which, when used in fact and in faith, shows the principalities, which argue and compete for the homage and service of men, to be the accomplices of death, offering only the transitory comforts of false gods. And, by the same gift, the Church is born into a freedom to be and to live in this world, amidst all the guiles of death, as the example and model of the whole of life as it is and is to be in the reconciliation of the whole world.

The Church as Church, the Church living in and by the freedom bestowed in Pentecost, is the foretaste and fore-runner—the priest (or representative) and prophet—of the reconciled society. The Church as Church is the image of God's own Kingdom, of the Eschaton. The Church as Church is the new nation, the true society, the holy com-munity, living here and now in the midst of death, aware but quite unafraid of all the powers of death, fully realistic about the present age upon which death and the servants of death intrude and over which they pretend to rule. In-deed, the Church lives in an estate of actual reconciliation with God and within the Word of God, embracing, thereby, the reconciliation of every member with and within him-self, with all other baptized members, and with all men and all things everywhere in the whole of creation. The Church as Church, in its very posture against all of the principalities and frail imitations of society which the principalities repre-

sent, is the real nation in which all mankind has been
offered citizenship by Christ himself, who is the sovereign
of this nation and whose Lordship the world longs for and
looks for even in the midst of the travail of bondage to
death.

In America the divided and separated churches seem to
have forgotten the identity and vocation of the Church
as the holy nation; in consequence, the witness of the several churches in the name of the Church is often inept, compromised, and profoundly confused. How shall the nation
—or any of the lesser principalities, for that matter—know
what it means to be a society under God, a true community
of reconciliation, if there is no visible witness in the existence and life of the Church as the exemplary holy nation
to behold? The divisions of the churches, where they dignify and appease the powers of death, where they represent
idolatry of one or another principality, inhibit the nation
from comprehending what its existence means in the sight
of God. These divisions hinder men from knowing what it
would mean to live in the City of Salvation instead of in
the city of death.

Apart from the distortion of the event of the holy—
which means perfect or whole or reconciled, not pure or
pietistic or moralistic conformity—nation by the disunities
of the churches, there are other reasons which account for
the absence in America of a sense of the Church as the
holy nation. For one thing, the radical emphasis for so
many generations in American Protestantism upon the individual and upon individualistic action as the main theme
and form of Christian witness has contributed to the loss

among church people of their identification and community with all baptized persons. There may be, in a particular sect or denomination, or sometimes in a specific parish or congregation, a very strong reality of common life, but too often this is oriented in an exclusory way, not only against secular society, but also against fellow Christians in other denominations or congregations. And, as often as not, the fact which unites such a sect or parish is not baptism into the Body of Christ and the company of the whole Church throughout the ages, but a peculiar credo pertaining to moral behavior, dress, class, race, social custom, or sometimes just the personality of a preacher or legends associated with the founder of the group. Churchly bodies such as these hardly commend themselves to the nation as models of the new society in Christ.

The American churches, furthermore, have forgotten the constitution of the Church as the holy nation and forerunner of the Kingdom because the churches here have so readily accommodated themselves to pluralism. They have prized the freedom given to the Church at Pentecost and vouchsafed to all Christians in baptism too little and too cheaply, while they prize extravagantly, if vainly, the public freedom accorded them by the nation to exist without much interference as religious institutions.

Yet the foretaste of the reconciled world which the Church is wherever the Church lives is not wholly absent from the American scene. One would hesitate gravely ever to identify it with any of the specific denominations or churches in America, having seen the marks which the denominational bodies bear in common with other principalities. While arguments may be made with some conviction that some denominations have originated in or represent an intention of reform and a catholic spirit which honors Christ, upholds his gospel, and respects his Church, it must be admitted, by and large, that the denominations in America are evidence of the work of death. Nevertheless, there are some congregations here and there (more, I am inclined to think, than the new criticism of the younger intelligentsia of the churches usually discerns) of several denominations which show in their faith and witness a comprehension and remarkable actualization of that which the Church is in the freedom of Pentecost.

And, in almost any congregation of virtually any denomination, one will find and can expect to find some Christian people who take seriously the authority of their baptism and live and work within the churches and in the world as emissaries of the Kingdom already present in the world which is the Church of Christ.

V. THE FREEDOM OF GOD

> Therefore let us leave the elementary
> doctrines of Christ and go on to ma-
> turity, not laying again a foundation
> of repentance from dead works and of
> faith toward God, with instruction
> about ablutions, the laying on of
> hands, the resurrection of the dead,
> and eternal judgment. And this we
> will do if God permits.
>
> *Hebrews 6:1-3*

The freedom of God in his ruling love for this world
in this world is not at all coincident with, contingent upon,
nor captive of the Church, much less so of the churches or
of individual Christians. If the Church or those within the
churches do not see and honor the freedom of God, if they
will not thus acknowledge and worship God, if they persist
in vain commendations of themselves instead of in gladness
in the Word of God, if they indulge in boasting witness to
themselves rather than bragging of their weakness to ex-
plain and attest God's grace and strength, if they conceive
of salvation as in part attributable to themselves and not
wholly the gift of God's initiative in this world, then God,
as has been the case before, in his terrible and magnificent

generosity with himself in the world, will simply find his own way of working his will and do without the churchly institutions and those who profess to be Christians and, so to speak, take over wholly himself the ministry of the Church.

This has, after all, happened before, as the Letter to the Hebrews so forcibly reminds. The Word of God was not absent from the history of this world before the birth of Jesus Christ. In fact and by the biblical testimony creation itself and all that is therein is given life in the utterance of that same Word disclosed in Jesus Christ. The Word of God is delivered in various ways and in diverse times in the history of the world, and in the gift of the Word within history a people of the Word, a peculiar nation, Israel, is called into being.

But the day comes to pass—long foreshadowed in the prophets and in the psalms; and later premonitive in the birth and earthly ministry of Jesus Christ, in the hostility of the worldly rulers to Christ, in his rejection at the hands of his own people and disciples, in his absolute abandonment—when Jesus Christ is, on the Cross, the embodiment within himself of God's people. The day, Good Friday, comes when Christ *is* Israel and there is no Israel as an authentic people of God save the remembrance, presence, and pioneer of that people in Christ himself. God, then and there, simply accepts the fact that he has been renounced and deserted by his own people, just as he was left by Adam, and perseveres in his own witness to himself as God which is his work of salvation.

In his time, by his own witness, according to his own will, by the generosity of his Godliness, in his compassion and forgiveness, in his freedom as God, God establishes in the aftermath of the resurrection of Christ, at Pentecost, a New Israel, the Church. This is the Body of Christ into which God elects all those who believe in him, that is, all those who beseech and trust the Word of God overwhelming the power of death in their own lives and in all the world.

But make no mistake about this: that God in the intercession of Christ in the world assembles and unites and ratifies a new nation, the Church, for himself and for his world does not mean that this same Church is thereby immune from the temptations of death, the wiles of the devil, the vanities common to all men, the substitution of idols for God, the glorification of self, forsaking the faith, apostasy, skepticism, heresy, and unbelief. God gives the Church a sufficient freedom to resist, refute, and renounce all of these things, but God's grace is not so cheap, unloving, and mechanistic as to shield the Church or its members from suffering the assaults of all of these things.

In short, the new and holy nation, the Church, which inherits the Cross of Christ, shares the gift of the Holy Spirit, and succeeds to the old nation, Israel, which had abdicated to death and advocated the Cross for Christ, is vulnerable to this day to every attack and tactic within the range and service of the power of death. And if, under such aggression, the Church as Church does not survive, even as Israel, then it may confidently be expected of God's mercy that he will again assume the task of the Church in witness to himself, just as God in Christ assumed the whole witness of Israel to God on the Cross.

The freedom of God in this world in his witness to himself is never mitigated, confounded, delayed, or precluded by the compromise of the integrity of the Church as his witness by the Church, by the churches, or among members of the Church. What is at stake may be the very existence of the Church as a people, or of a particular church body, or of a member of the Church, but what is never at stake is the efficacy of God's own witness to himself and, within that, to the given and true life of the whole world in reconciliation. What is at stake is not whether there will be an ample witness to the Word of God, but whether those who call themselves Christian and those who use the name of the Church will be deprived of the pleasure and prerogative of participating in God's witness to himself in this history.

THE WITNESS OF MERE PRESENCE

The problem which has always plagued and will always plague the Church and its members is the very problem of the Hebrews, not only before the ministry of Christ, but during his earthly ministry, and, as the Letter to the Hebrews shows, even after his resurrection. The problem is, simply, that of receiving the gift of the Word of God which is salvation from death itself and then, in one fashion or another, concealing from the world this gift which is first entrusted to the Church at Pentecost and to the Christian in baptism. The temptation before the Church, and thence before the churches and the Christians, is to receive and then covet rather than proclaim and share his gift. The peril is that the gift is disclosed to the world only on condition that the world admire the trustee of the gift rather than the Giver. The world is then profoundly misled and considers the gift as other than what it is.

One example of that is where the Church tries to confine the gospel to standards of conformity in behavior or belief set up by the Church or some sects of the Church. Thus, in the first Israel, the people of God received the gift of the Word of God in the commandments delivered through Moses. The people heard, for instance, in that specific revelation of God's Word, that "thou shalt not kill." They thereafter engaged in defining and limiting the acts and omissions which constitute killing in order to dispense to themselves and promise to other men a means of easy obedience and apparent fidelity to the Word of God.

What actually results is a restriction and alteration of the Word of God into something so soft or simplistic that most men can literally obey the commandment and thus justify themselves without any need of God's grace as judgment or forgiveness. Thus, killing is reduced to certain definitions of actual homicide resulting in death by intentional or negligent violence of a person or persons. But overlooked in such a tempering with God's Word are all the meanings of killing beyond the conventional forms of murder and manslaughter which are contained and enacted in our ordinary alienation from one another in, as Christ himself reminds in the Sermon on the Mount, the mere anger of one towards another.

In the Sermon when Christ explicitly discusses the old law, he is not adding to or altering the dimensions of the Word of God disclosed therein; he is rather recalling for

Israel the original dimensions of the commandments. He is restoring the truth of the Word in the commandments and exposing how much the Word had been distorted and restricted after its revelation through Moses.

Who is there, after all, among men who has not killed in one way or another and does not fall, therefore, within the judgment of the Word of God? Who is there who does not need God's mercy, even though he does not want it or would prefer to earn his own salvation? Whenever you regard another human being as less than yourself, you convict yourself of killing him. Whenever a parent exploits an offspring by imposing his or her own personality or aspirations upon the child, murder is done. Whenever sex is primitive aggrandizement of one by another, someone is killed. Whenever a man dishonors his own God-given life by anger, greed, hate, envy, insult, or malice, he takes his own life no less than a suicide. All men are not murderers in the sense of violent, negligent, or passionate deadly assault on another's life, but no man is innocent of violating the commandment of the Word of God not to kill.

Such a radical and inclusive scope applies as well to the other commandments. As a result, there is no man who is not liable to judgment, and there is none without need of forgiveness. This is just as true of men today as it was to the Israelites who listened to Moses or the hearers of the Sermon on the Mount.

The Word of God is belittled when in the Church or in one of the churches the Word is construed in a fashion that makes obedience to the Word of God not dependence upon grace but a convenient moralistic, pietistic, or ritualistic conformity. Some of the common examples in American churches of such conformity do not have the dignity of an even colorable biblical basis. That is the case with those sects which teach that the practice of the Christian life chiefly consists of abstention from smoking, drinking, and dancing; those which make a fetish about customs of diet and dress; those which regard attendance in churchly rites and ceremonies magically or mechanistically; or those which disregard the wholeness of the Bible and select from it the fragments which seem to reinforce and condone what they prefer to say and do. None of these practices has any inherent efficacy to save a man from the power of death, nor will any of them enable a man to escape the fullness of God's judgment. And all such efforts only imitate the disrespect shown for the Word of God in the earlier days of the old Israel.

In other words, there are these problems which entice and tempt the Church and the members of the Church: to legislate the gospel; to equate obedience to God's freedom with loyalty to the churchly institutions; to adulterate the Word of God by exaggeration of the importance of the Church in the economy of salvation; to make the witness of Christ himself contingent upon the Church when, in fact, the existence of the Church is wholly derived from the intercession of Christ on the Cross which is at once the inaugural of the resurrection, the foundation of Pentecost, and that to which the baptized are already beneficiaries. The issue is the Church usurping God instead of worshiping God in service to the world.

The Church and the Christians are too much afraid of

the gospel. They suppose that there is something still to be added to the work of salvation besides just the proclamation and celebration of the event. They think that to be a Christian one must do something beyond what already has been done by God in Christ, not only for Christians, but for all men in all the world.

The trouble is that Christians too often suppose that God's work in this world is unaccomplished without them. The truth is that no man, even the Christian, has any life or security against death unless he relies wholly upon the finality and perfection of God's work in this world.

Even more bluntly put: the Christian, and the whole company which is the Church, need not worry about what is to be done. The task is, rather, to live within the victory of all that has been done by God. For the Christian the issue is not so much about what he does in this world but about who he is in this world. There is no serious distinction between who the Christian is and what he does, between being and doing. These are virtually the same.

It is similar, I notice, in some other realms of life. One would not think, for the most obvious example, of distinguishing being and doing in one's relationship with another person whom one loves. If you love another (and we are not talking about mere erotic infatuation or something less) and if you and the one you love confront each other and engage in some act of love, you would not think of speaking or describing what you do and have done together in any different way than as you would speak of who you are in relation to one another. Who you are to one another and what you do with one another are, as it were, the same thing, inseparable and indistinguishable; one cannot be referred to without the other. There is, in love, a unity of being and doing.

It is something like that in the Christian faith. The Christian, contrary to the counsels of the pietistic and moralistic and the example of the Pharisees, but wholly consistent with the witness of the prophets and faithful to the wisdom and freedom of primitive Christians, senses no separation in his own existence between who he is and what he does. These are indivisible. They are one and the same. The Christian is given in Christ a new life in which his wholeness as a person is restored to him, and so radical is his integrity as a person that the mere presence of a Christian in a place (and by the same token the mere presence of a congregation of Christians in some place) is the witness.

Such integrity, such a unity of being and doing, makes the task of Christians and of the Church in witness a very modest one. The Christian commends the Word of God to other men by the reality of his own new life. The Church commends the gospel to the world by the very event of the Church's life as a holy nation. Christians and the Church are both free in witness from any need, compulsion, or concern to commend themselves as such to men or to the world. Thus, they are free from pleasing men or appeasing the principalities of the world.

In witness Christians are even free from anxieties about how God will one day judge their specific decisions and actions. The Christian trusts God so much and honors his being so much that he does not entangle himself in trying to anticipate God's judgment or to displace that judgment with his own. The Christian knows, moreover, that God's witness to himself in this world is not impaired by the weakness of Christians or falsehood in the Church.

The essential attribute of the witness of mere presence is radical confidence in the vitality of God's own witness to himself. Such confidence is so extreme that the Christian witness is not self-conscious and calculating, but selfless and spontaneous. In fact, the witness of the Christian is never really *his* witness as such, but is rather his affirmation of and surrender to and participation in the witness of God to himself in each and every event of history. To speak of the Christian, therefore, as a member incorporated into the Body of Christ is no quaint figure of speech; it is a concrete description of the loss or death of one's old identity and the entering into a new life and identity in Christ.

In witness, in other words, the Christian does not suffer any concern about his own justification (that was the affliction of the Hebrews in the early Church) but entrusts his justification to God's abundant mercy. Thus free from this most deadly fear, he goes about rejoicing. That *is* the witness.

By the same token, the Church, where it is a witness to God, does not seek first the preservation of the Church or the conservation of the possessions, reputation, and power of the institutions of the Church; that was the corruption of the old Israel. The Church leaves all such things to God's disposal, and, thus free from this most worldly anxiety, gathers to celebrate the presence of the Word of God in the world. That *is* the witness.

If any complain that this understanding of witness as

presence is one which makes witness very difficult, involving always the death to self which is the gift of life in Christ, then let it be said that it is futile for any man to feign to justify himself, especially in the name of witness. I cannot save myself. How is it then any obstacle if I am justified by God's freedom, as a gift?

To such complaint, let it be answered that any view which presupposes a separation in the Christian life, or in the Church's life, between being and doing only ridicules the new birth which is given in baptism and dishonors the gift of Pentecost. To this complaint, the answer is that any understanding of witness which considers it to be essentially an origination of the Church or of a member of the Church rather than the acceptance of and participation in God's witness to himself plainly demeans the stature of God. What is really complained of, in this case, is a distrust of God's grace.

THE WITNESS IN WORSHIP

Witness which has integrity in the gospel is always an inherently sacramental event—a confession and celebration of God's freely given and wholly sufficient reconciling action in Christ, to which nothing can be added or amended nor anything compromised or taken away. Knowing the presence of the Word of God in the world, being made a new person by the power of that Word, the Christian's task is to so enjoy the Word in the world as to attest the veracity of the Word of God for all men in any and every event.

The characteristic and common form of the sacramental

life, which is a unity of being and doing, is the celebration of the gospel in the congregation gathered in worship. The Church engages in observances and rites: the Church baptizes a new person into the community of the Word of God; the Church discerns and partakes of the Word in the Lord's Supper; the Church listens to the Word in the Bible and hears it proclaimed in preaching. In all of these customary and inherited ways, the Church recalls and recites the gospel and celebrates the remembrance of all that God has done.

At the same time and in the same ways in the same celebration the Church anticipates with gladness and eagerness the final reconciliation of the whole of creation. The Church announces, heralds, and exemplifies the promise of the gospel for all men in all the world for all time.

The celebration of the Word in the congregation's sacramental life in worship is not only an event of remembrance and preview: the Church is as well engaged in celebrating the reconciliation known now and already within the Church on behalf of the world. The celebration in Holy Baptism, the Eucharist, and the preaching of the Word in the congregation (which, though not universally designated as an historic sacrament, obviously and essentially partakes of the nature of a sacrament) is a festival of the event of reconciliation already taking place in the midst of history.

Yet bear in mind that the forms of the very same sacraments may be perverted into necromancy, as St. Paul admonished the Church in Corinth (I Cor. 10:14-21), where what transpires is not the spontaneous, existential expression and representation of the reality of the Church as the people already reconciled with themselves, with each other, and with the whole of creation by God's mercy and judgment. Where the sacraments do not represent the unity of being and doing in the Church, they become idols, no different from the other principalities of tradition and institution in the world; participation in and use of the sacraments then becomes idolatrous.

Mere rite or ceremony, observed and glorified for its own sake and becoming forms without faith, is a much more common sort of profanity, taking the Lord's name in vain, than the profanity so typical of ordinary speech on the streets. Such profanity and such idolatry is present wherever participation in the sacraments is occasioned by superstition, sentimentality, self-aggrandizement, the desire to appease God, or some mechanical understanding of the sacraments.

There are many instances of just these things in the congregations of contemporary Christendom. For some the Mass is regarded as magic; for some the sacraments are considered indulgences; some church people attend worship services out of a sense of duty or obligation in the hope that they will thereby earn some benefit or in the fear that their absence will bring down the scorn of God. It is more likely that they just invite the displeasure of the clergy and the judgmental gossip of their neighbors.

When the forms of the sacraments become idols and the sacraments become radically secularized, the world is misled about the meaning and grandeur of God's work and bewildered about the scope and substance of the Christian faith. Perhaps it is this profaning of the sacraments which explains the superstitious use of such Christian symbols as medals and mustard seed remembrances as good luck charms.

Because idolatry is a constant peril, because the sacraments represent more than remembrance and preview, because the whole of the Christian life and witness is sacramental and informed and nurtured through the sacraments, it is imperative to be concrete about what happens in the celebration of the gospel in the common sacraments. It suits the economy of this book to discuss with particularity, illustratively, only the sacrament of the Holy Communion, though, in principle, what is affirmed about the Eucharist can as well be said of Holy Baptism and of the preaching of the Word of God in the congregation.

The celebration of the gospel in the Holy Communion is a thanksgiving, *eucharistis,* to God for the gospel. The Eucharist is the acknowledgment of who God is and of what he has done for the world; the Eucharist glorifies God, to be specific, because *he is God.* In giving thanks and praise to God, the congregation is identified not only with the whole Church throughout the ages, but with the whole of creation. Though creation is ruined, it is still sustained by God in ruin, and in spite of its ruin creation points to God. Though men, under the power of sin, hate God, when they come unto themselves they praise him. This the Church knows and celebrates and, on behalf of all men and the whole of creation, the Church gives thanks to God in the Eucharist.

The Church's celebration in the Eucharist is therefore intercessory. The congregation gives thanks for itself, for the whole Church, for all men, and for the whole world.

To intercede for others is not sentimental identification with those in need because of sickness, trouble, sorrow, or any other adversity, but solemn reliance upon the grace of God. Intercession means to stand before God in willingness to accept the burden of another in freedom, to take the place of another in his need. The Church dares to take on the affliction and suffering of the world because of its knowledge that God's love endures. The congregation knows God is faithful. When it intercedes for the world the Church is, with particular clarity, the Body of Christ sharing his ministry, for Christ has made the consummate intercession for the whole world.

Intercession has nothing to do with persuading God to do what men would like done; it is no part either of self-inducement, bolstering men to do what they want to do. Intercession has nothing to do with men's will for themselves, but only with God's will for the world. Intercession is the freedom of Christians to suffer with and for others as a witness to the world that in his suffering for the world, God has overcome suffering. Intercession is a celebration of this good news which is God's will for the world.

Because intercession in the Eucharist is, in the end, a petition that God's will be done, it is an acknowledgment by the congregation of their identity as men, subject, as other men, to the power of sin. Christians acknowledge God in thanksgiving; they acknowledge themselves in penitence. Contrition is integral to the celebration of the gospel. Penitence is not, however, an act which earns for Christians a place at the table of the Lord. Rather, penitence is an act of love for God. The perfection of love of God by men is not the attainment of some standard of merit required or demanded by God, but the wholeness, the completeness of our gift of ourselves and all that we are as sinful men to him. Repentance and penitence are involved in the wholeness of surrender to God, in perfectly loving him, and it is reliance upon the fullness of his love, upon the sufficiency of that love in expiating sin.

Now the Supper of the Lord takes place; the gospel is celebrated; the Church in the congregation is alive; now there is a Holy Communion. The congregation comes to the Lord in praise and thanksgiving, in intercession and petition, in penitence and contrition. The celebration of the gospel in the Holy Communion is the oblation of the congregation, the offering to God, in the only full and appropriate response of men to his redemptive gift of himself. Here are returned all that he first gave men: these elements of bread and wine and these alms, in evidence of God's gift to men of dominion over the rest of creation; this gathered congregation, in testimony of God's gift to men of community; and "our selves, our souls and bodies," in honor of God's gift of life to each and every man. Everything is given to God that God first gave to the world. In this celebration of the gospel *the very event* is taking place in the midst of history; God is reconciling the world to himself; he is reigning in his world; God is with his people, and his people worship him as God. Thereby the message of reconciliation is published and proclaimed.

When the congregation worships God, God is vindicated before all men; the world may see who God is and believe what he has done for the world in Christ. In the Holy

Communion, the new community in Christ, the Christian society is manifest in history as over against all other nations and all the societies men make as a witness that the true hope for community is in Christ.

OBEDIENCE UNTO DEATH

Christians live in the world and bear and embody the message of reconciliation in the world, not only as the gathered congregation but also in dispersion, scattered in the world, taking part in its ordinary life and work. This is, by the way, the experience of every Christian, just as much for the priest as for the layman. The office and function of the priest is in the administration of the sacraments and the nurture of the congregation; all of the manifold activities of the ordained ministry which are not inherent to this office are, in principle, secular occupations of the clergy no different from a layman's secular work.

When the congregation disperses and Christians go out into the world, the conflict between the Church and the world becomes very explicitly, so to speak, personalized. A Christian lives from day to day in the tension between Church and world, between Christ and Caesar, between grace and law, between salvation and sin, between life and death, and between freedom and bondage.

To live in that tension worship in the congregation and witness in the world must be integral to one another. There is no solitary witness of a Christian in the world, isolated from the congregation, because the sacramental worship in the congregation is the comprehensive and exemplary

Christian witness in the world. Any so-called Christian action in the world is void in the inception if it is cut off from the informing support, edification, love, and nurture of the celebration of the gospel in the congregation. In reality, the Christian bears the tension between the gospel and the world in radical and transforming witness only because he participates in the event of the congregation. It is that event which enables him to witness while dispersed in the world.

In terms of daily work, which is the most ordinary scene of his witness in the world's life, a Christian works in the world just as any man does. He has some job, as a lawyer or a laundryman, teacher or teller. He is related in work to the material of his work, to the discipline of his profession or occupation, to those with whom he works, to those for whom he works, and to those against whom he works. But the gospel makes this difference: the Christian knows that men have lost dominion over the rest of creation and that in its place is toil, pain, transience, alienation, and, in fact, bondage to death itself.

But the Christian in his daily work is no more a slave to death. He has been set free by the grace of God in Christ. He is free to appropriate the material and relationships of his work to worship, glorify, and offer to God. His oblation in work, like his participation in the oblation of the congregation, is manifold: it is his acknowledgment of God in praise and thanksgiving and his acknowledgment of himself as a man in repentance and penitence. It includes his intercession, his freedom to share the burdens of his fellow workers, clients, employers, or competitors.

In short, the whole of Christian life, both that within the gathered congregation and that in dispersion in the world, is sacramental, and the structure, relationships, meaning, and style of life is the same whether the Christian is participating in the esoteric life of the congregation in worship or is involved in the practical life of the world. The sacramental life of the congregation informs, enables, and sets the precedent for the sacramental life of the individual Christian in his daily work and witness in society.

But the latter is at the same time that which the Christian brings to the oblation of the whole congregation. That is why, incidentally, it is fitting that money has become the virtually exclusive tangible symbol used in the Offertory. For nothing more clearly represents the involvement of the Christian in the common life of American society than money. Nothing is more worldly and vulgar than money. Nothing, therefore, is more appropriate to show that what is being offered to God is the whole of our lives, not just that which we deem acceptable to him or which seems to us creative or competently done, or which has been well received of men, but also all that which is incomplete, which is not praised, which is not known, or which is painful or unpleasant to behold. The offering of money is a sign that the oblation of the Christian does not have to have any particular merit or worth of its own, but it has to be complete, encompassing the whole life of that Christian in the world.

This is how integral the sacramental life in congregation and in dispersion in the world are to one another. The sacramental events in the congregation exemplify the witness of Christians in the world; the witness in the world gives content to the forms of sacramental life in the congregation. Each authorizes and authenticates the other.

All this is not for the sake of the Christians, not for their justification either individually or as the Church, but for the sake of the world, for other men. A Christian is free in his knowledge and experience of the love of God for the world to love the world himself. A Christian does not love another man for himself—else how would one love his own enemy? —but for his sake, that is, because of what God has done for him. A Christian loves another man in a way that affirms his true humanity, vouchsafed for him and for all men in the resurrection.

The life of the Christian both within and outside the gathered congregation is sacramental. But of what practical significance is that for a Christian in his daily decisions and actions? The witness which is obedience to God's freedom is one which celebrates the gospel, but of what guidance is that in choosing a job, casting a ballot, raising a child, facing illness, spending money, or any of the other ordinary issues of daily existence?

The short answer to such questions is that the witness which is truly obedience to the freedom of God means freedom without measure for men. That means that the Christian is free to take the world and every aspect of its existence, every person and every principality, seriously. Out of respect, as it were, for God's creation and for both the incarnation and the Holy Spirit, the Christian deals with history in this world just as it is and makes decisions in terms of the actual events in which he is involved as they happen. In doing so he knows that there is no place in which his presence is forbidden, no person whom he may not welcome, no work in which he may not engage, no situation into which he may not enter, without first of all finding that he has been preceded, so to speak, by the Word of God.

The Christian does not need to construct any hypothetical presuppositions, any theoretics of decision, after the manner of the Greeks, the Hebrews in the early Church, or the later pietists of one sort or another. To do that denigrates the freedom of God in judging the world and all the decisions and actions of men and nations in the way that it pleases him to do, by enthroning some principles of decision in the place of God. Such ethics, in any of their varieties, are no armor against the realities of the world, the temptations of the flesh, or the power of death; they are only means of hiding from all of these.

There are, to be sure, certain marks of the ministry and witness of the Church and of Christians in the world: radicality, penitence, intercession for the outcast, and the like; but that is not the same thing as some legalistic ethics. Such ethics have no saving power for the world for they invariably are the expression of the self-interest of the very persons and principalities which adhere to them and attempt to implement and enforce them. Nor do they have any efficacy in justifying those beholden to them.

Nor will any such scheme of ethics save any man from God's judgment. All men and nations are judged in all their ethics, motives, decisions, and actions by God himself. No one aids him in this office, and no one can take another's place, nor can one be spared God's judgment by any other means, though that be the intention of all ethics. That being so, the freedom of the Christian consists of his acceptance of the fact that his own justification by the working of God's freedom relieves him even of the anxiety over how he is judged by God.

The Christian goes about—wherever he be, which may be anywhere, whomever he is with, which may be anyone —edified and upheld by the sacramental community which is the Church in the congregation. He is ready to face whatever is to be faced knowing that the only enemy is the power of death, whatever form or appearance death may take. He is confident that the Word of God has already gone before him. Therefore he can live and act, whatever the circumstances, without fear of or bondage to either his own death or the works of death in the world. He is enabled and authorized by the gift of the Holy Spirit to the Church and to himself in baptism to expose all that death has done and can do, rejoicing in the freedom of God which liberates all men, all principalities, all things from bondage to death.

That being so, the Christian is free to give his own life to the world, to anybody at all, even to one who does not know about or acknowledge the gift, even to one whom the world would regard as unworthy of the gift. He does so without reserve, compromise, hesitation, or prudence, but with modesty, assurance, truth, and serenity. That being so, the Christian is free, within the freedom of God, to be obedient unto his own death.